MW00759836

READING NONFICTION 2

- Animals in the News
- Sports Spectaculars
- Inventors and Inventions
- Historic American Places

READING in context

READING *in context*

PRACTICAL READING 1

PRACTICAL READING 2

READING NONFICTION 1

READING NONFICTION 2

READING FICTION 1

READING FICTION 2

SADDLEBACK
PUBLISHING·INC.

Three Watson
Irvine, CA 92618-2767

E-Mail: info@sdlback.com
Website: www.sdlback.com

Development and Production: Laurel Associates, Inc.
Cover Design: Elisa Ligon
Interior Illustrations: Ginger Slonaker

ISBN 1-56254-192-7

Printed in the United States of America
05 04 03 02 01   9 8 7 6 5 4 3 2 1

CONTENTS

INTRODUCTION

A NOTE TO THE STUDENT

Skillful readers have many advantages in life. While they are in school, they obviously get better grades. But the benefits go far beyond the classroom. Good readers are also good thinkers, problem-solvers, and decision-makers. They can avoid many of the problems and frustrations that unskilled readers miss out on. In short, good readers have a much greater chance to be happy and successful in all areas of their lives.

READING IN CONTEXT is an all-around skill-building program. Its purpose is to help you achieve your goals in life by making you a better reader. Each of the six worktexts has been designed with your needs and interests in mind. The reading selections are engaging and informative—some lighthearted and humorous, others quite serious and thought-provoking. The follow-up exercises teach the essential skills and concepts that lead to reading mastery.

We suggest that you thumb through the book before you begin work. Read the table of contents. Notice that each of the four units is based on a unifying theme. Then take a moment to look through the four lessons that make up each theme-based unit. Scan one of the *Before reading* paragraphs that introduces a lesson. Glance at the *Preview* and *Review* pages that begin and end each unit. "Surveying" this book (or any book) in this informal way is called *prereading*. It helps you "get a fix on" the task ahead by showing you how the book is organized. Recognizing patterns is an important thinking skill in itself. And in this case it will make you more comfortable and confident as you begin your work.

Happy reading!

ANIMALS IN THE NEWS

LESSON 1: Bring Back the Grizzlies

LESSON 2: Eagles Back from the Brink

LESSON 3: Penguins at Risk

LESSON 4: The Great White Shark

When you complete this unit, you will be able to answer questions like these:

- *Why does the great white shark never stop swimming?*

- *What recent disaster threatened an entire species of penguins?*

- *How can you tell the difference between a bald eagle and a vulture?*

- *How many square miles does a grizzly bear need for "roaming room"?*

PRETEST

Write **T** or **F** to show whether you think each statement is *true* or *false*.

1. _____ A pesticide called DDT was banned because it damaged the eggs of some birds.

2. _____ In the past 200 years, the grizzly bear population in the western United States has decreased 98 percent.

3. _____ Great white sharks almost never lift their heads out of the water.

4. _____ Penguins lost their ability to fly millions of years ago.

5. _____ Oil spills from big ships can usually be cleaned up in a day or two.

6. _____ Scientists think the great white shark doesn't enjoy the taste of human flesh.

Pretest answers: 1. T 2. T 3. F 4. T 5. F 6. T

BRING BACK THE GRIZZLIES

Before reading . . .

The Bitterroot National Forest in Idaho is historic "grizzly country." But not even one grizzly bear has been sighted there in 70 years. This lesson presents arguments for and against restoring the grizzly to its former home.

A DWINDLING POPULATION

In 1806, explorers Lewis and Clark estimated that some 50,000 grizzlies roamed the western United States. Then came the trappers, hunters, ranchers, and homesteaders. Now, there are some 400–600 bears in the Yellowstone ecosystem. There are another 500 or so in Glacier National Park in Montana. And about 50,000 grizzlies are thought to live in Alaska and Canada.

Since 1975, the grizzly bear has been on the federal government's list of threatened species. "Without the grizzly," one official said, "we've got a watered-down ecosystem." So the U.S. Fish and Wildlife Service has proposed plans to bring the grizzly back to Idaho.

The plan is to introduce five bears to the Bitterroot Mountains each year for five consecutive years. It's a small start. Wildlife experts point out that the grizzly has a slow reproductive cycle. They say it would take more than 100 years to reach the projected goal of 300 bears in the Bitterroot range.

Federal biologists say the Bitterroots provide an ideal habitat for the grizzlies. Its vast range provides plenty of room for the bears—each of which needs up to 600 square miles in which to roam. And the area is well-stocked with the foods that comprise 90 percent of a bear's diet. These foods include tubers, wild truffles, glacier lilies, wild berries, ants, and grubs.

Certain safeguards are built into the plan. Only bears having no history of conflict with humans would be transplanted into Idaho. And each bear would be tagged and equipped with a radio tracking device. This would make it easier for wildlife management officials to monitor the bears' movements.

The grizzly reintroduction plan is not a sure thing, however. It must first be approved by the Director of the U.S. Fish and Wildlife Service and the U.S. Secretary of the Interior. And then they must find the $2 million needed to fund the first five years of the program.

Keep the Grizzlies Out!

The grizzly's return to Idaho could be blocked by public protest, private lawsuits, or direct government intervention. Many elected officials in Idaho join ranchers in opposing the proposal.

"Bears spend 99.9 percent of their time staying away from humans," says the coordinator of the bear recovery plan. "And if bears do see a human, all they want is to get away." Yet even so, he admits that *some* "nuisance incidents" would be likely to occur with the bears' return. Such incidents, he estimates, could average 37 a year—with the grizzlies killing about six cattle and 25 sheep annually.

Many residents of central Idaho worry about the threat to human safety. Idaho Governor Dirk Kempthorne reacted to the plan in no uncertain terms. "This is perhaps the first federal land-management action in history likely to result in the injury or death of members of the public."

Some environmentalists argue against the plan as well. They say it *doesn't go far enough* to protect the grizzlies. If they had their way, the status of the grizzly would be upgraded from "threatened" to "endangered." Under that designation, the grizzly would have automatic protection under the Endangered Species Act.

WHY THE BITTERROOTS?

The proposed relocation site is a 5,785-square-mile area in the heart of the Selway-Bitterroot Wilderness. This land is in east-central Idaho and adjacent Montana. It is the largest remaining expanse of federal land in the lower 48 states. And it is also one of only six places in the United States suitable for grizzlies.

COMPREHENSION

Use proper names from the reading to answer the questions. Don't forget that proper names must be capitalized!

1. What federal agency has proposed the bear relocation plan?

    _____

2. Which two 19th century explorers saw thousands of grizzly bears in the western United States?

    _____

3. What federal act protects animals in danger of extinction?

    _____

4. In which two states is the Selway-Bitterroot Wilderness located?

    _____

5. What two national parks in the lower 48 states are still "home" to grizzly bears?

    _____

FACT OR OPINION?

Write **F** or **O** to show whether each statement is a *fact* or an *opinion*.

1. _____ The U.S. Secretary of the Interior should be more concerned about polar bears than grizzly bears.

2. _____ In the past 200 years, about 48,000 grizzlies have disappeared from the lower 48 states.

3. _____ It is cruel to force a grizzly to wear a radio tracking device.

4. _____ There might still be a few undiscovered grizzlies living in Idaho's wilderness.

5. _____ If vegetables comprise 90 percent of a grizzly's diet, the rest of its diet must include meat, fish, and insects.

6. _____ Normally, grizzly bears want nothing to do with humans.

7. _____ States that are *adjacent* must border one another.

8. _____ A "watered-down" ecosystem is missing one or more important elements.

PUZZLER

Use the clues to help you solve the crossword puzzle. Answers are words that complete the sentences.

ACROSS

1. Each bear needs 600 square miles in which to _____.

5. The relocation site is a huge _____ of federal land.

7. Many _____ of central Idaho worry about human safety.

8. A bear's diet includes _____ and grubs.

¹R		²A			³F	
⁴F						
	⁵E			⁶S		
⁷R			E			
		⁸A				

DOWN

2. Montana is _____ to the state of Idaho.

3. The first _____ years of the program would cost $2 million.

4. The grizzly is on the _____ government's list of threatened species.

6. The proposed _____ covers 5,785 square miles.

IRREGULAR PLURALS

Write the *plural* form (names more than one) of each word from the reading.

1. berry _____

2. sheep _____

3. grizzly _____

4. species _____

5. lily _____

6. agency _____

SPELLING

Circle the correctly spelled word in each group.

1. goverment   government   govermant

2. secretary   secretery   secratary

3. coordinater   co-ordinator   coordinator

4. nuisance   nuisence   nuicanse

SENTENCE COMPLETION

Unscramble the **boldface** words from the reading to complete the sentences.

1. An **SOMESTYCE** _____ is the community of plants and animals that live together in a certain environment.

2. **BRUTES** _____ are thick underground stems such as potatoes.

3. A **SUNCAINE** _____ is something that causes trouble or bother.

4. An animal's **ANGER** _____ is the amount of open land it needs to comfortably move around.

5. To **NALPSTARTN** _____ an animal is to move it to another place.

6. There are only six **BLAUSTIE** _____ locations for grizzlies in the United States.

VOCABULARY

Circle a letter to show the meaning of the **boldface** word or words.

1. Idaho's governor reacted to the plan **in no uncertain terms**.

   a. as if he hadn't quite made up his mind

   b. in a way that couldn't be misunderstood

   c. using technical terms no one understood

10

2. The grizzly bear has a slow **reproductive cycle**.

    a. rate of   b. unwillingness   c. very long
       producing   to mate in   term of
       offspring   certain years   pregnancy

3. The Bitterroots make an ideal **habitat** for the grizzly.

    a. habits that   b. custom of   c. place where
       ensure long   returning to   an animal is
       life   the same place   usually found

4. Some **environmentalists** are not in favor of the bear relocation plan.

    a. those who work   b. people who   c. important
       to protect natural   pollute the   government
       resources   environment   officials

5. Five bears will be introduced each year for five **consecutive** years.

    a. guaranteed   b. in order   c. in an every-
       by the chief   without a   other-year
       executive   break   pattern

6. Wild **truffles** and glacier lilies are part of the grizzly's diet.

    a. chocolate candies   b. small pigs   c. underground fungus

SYLLABLES

Divide the words from the reading into *syllables* (separate sounds).

intervention	biologists	federal	introduce
homesteaders	automatic	habitat	

1. _____ / _____ / _____   _____ / _____ / _____

   _____ / _____ / _____   _____ / _____ / _____

2. _____ / _____ / _____ / _____

   _____ / _____ / _____ / _____

   _____ / _____ / _____ / _____

EAGLES BACK FROM THE BRINK

Before reading . . .

In the early 1970s, the bald eagle was on the brink of extinction. People feared that our proud national symbol might one day vanish entirely. But now this once endangered bird is becoming a fairly common sight along the Potomac.

A PROUD SYMBOL

The eagle has long been used as a symbol of power, courage, and freedom. In 1787, the newly formed United States took the bald eagle as its emblem. Its picture is on the Great Seal of the United States, the president's flag, some coins, and paper money. The U.S. emblem shows the bald eagle with outspread wings and a shield on its breast. It holds an olive branch in one foot and a sheaf of arrows in the other.

Numbers Are Rebounding

Sightseers have always loved to visit Mount Vernon, George Washington's estate on the Potomac River. And these days, if they're lucky, they may see something unexpected and wonderful there—a bald eagle swooping out of the trees!

After the near extinction of the bald eagle, such sightings are becoming more common around Chesapeake Bay. In 1970, there were only 80 to 90 breeding pairs in the region. Today, there are about 600 pairs as well as hundreds of chicks. This recovery began when bald eagles were listed as an endangered species in 1973. But the revival of these fierce raptors may decline again if their habitat shrinks.

The director of the Center for Conservation at the College of William and Mary in Williamsburg, Virginia, has issued a grim warning. He says that the bald eagle's future is directly threatened by real estate development. The truth of his contention is obvious. Where mansions, docks, and boats crowd the shoreline, there are no eagles. On undeveloped stretches of the shore, however, eagles roost in the trees and dive for fish.

When the United States was founded, there were as many as a half-million eagles in North America. By 1963, there were fewer than 500 breeding pairs in the lower 48 states. The decline was mainly attributed to the loss of prey and habitat. Another significant factor was the widespread use of DDT—a pesticide that causes female eagles to lay brittle eggs. DDT was banned in the United States in 1972, beginning the recovery. But have the bald eagles *fully* recovered?

The fact is that the sensitive eagles just don't mix well with humans. Can they withstand the growing human population along the Potomac? Only time will tell.

SHOULD FEDERAL PROTECTION BE RELAXED?

In 1995, the bald eagle's status was downgraded from "endangered" to "threatened." Now the U.S. Fish and Wildlife Service wants to remove the bird from the endangered species list altogether. No decision about the bald eagle has been made as yet. But fewer than 30 species have ever been completely removed from the endangered species list.

North American Eagles

There are only two eagle species that live in North America—the bald eagle and the golden eagle. Except for the California condor, eagles are the largest American bird of prey. The condor, however, is a vulture. You can tell a flying eagle from a vulture by looking at its head. The eagle's head is large and covered with feathers. The vulture's head is small and bare.

The Bald Eagle

Except for a few white spots, young bald eagles are gray or smoky brown. The head, neck, and tail do not turn white until the bird is three or four years old. Feathers grow on the legs to within an inch of the toes. The bill, feet, and bare parts of the legs are bright yellow. Males and females have the same coloring.

A male bald eagle weighs about eight pounds and is about 35 inches long. It has a wingspread of about seven feet. Females are usually larger. Their length may be as great as 42 inches, and their weight about 12 pounds. The female's wingspread is about eight feet.

Adapted for Hunting

The bald eagle has a strong bill and powerful claws, or talons. The bill is nearly as long as the head. The upper half of the bill curves down sharply over the lower. The eagle uses its strong toes and talons to grasp its prey. It eats meat, including many small mammals, reptiles, and birds. But fish is perhaps the favorite meal of the bald eagle.

COMPREHENSION

Use information from the reading to help you answer the questions.

1. What two eagle species live in North America?

   _____

2. What parts of a bald eagle are bright yellow?

   _____

3. Along what river has the population
   of eagles increased?   _____

4. What status does the U.S. Fish and Wildlife Service *now*
   recommend for the bald eagle?

   _____

5. In what year was the bald eagle selected
   as the emblem of the United States?   _____

6. About 200 years ago, how many eagles
   were thought to live in the United States? _____

ALPHABETICAL ORDER

List the words from the reading in alphabetical order on the lines below.

vulture	symbol	condor	recovery	swooping
factor	extinction	reptiles	significant	revival

1. _____   6. _____

2. _____   7. _____

3. _____   8. _____

4. _____   9. _____

5. _____   10. _____

SYLLABLES

Divide the words from the reading into *syllables* (separate sounds).

conservation	extinction	sightseers

1. _____ / _____ / _____   _____ / _____ / _____

2. _____ / _____ / _____ / _____

PUZZLER

Use the clues to help you solve the crossword puzzle. Answers are
words that complete the sentences.

ACROSS

2. The bald eagle's head is covered with _____.

6. The eagle is a _____ of power, courage, and freedom.

7. Conservationists issued a _____ warning about the effects of real estate development.

8. The eagle's talons make it well _____ for hunting.

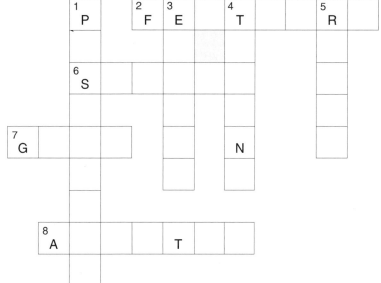

DOWN

1. DDT is a _____ that affects the eagle's eggs.

3. The bald eagle is the _____ of the United States.

4. An eagle's claws are called _____.

5. Eagles _____ in trees on the undeveloped shoreline.

15

SPELLING

Circle the correctly spelled word in each group.

1. smokey   smoky   smokie

2. sensitive   sensative   sensitave

3. entirly   entirelly   entirely

CRITICAL THINKING

Write **T** or **F** to show whether each statement is *true* or *false.*

1. _____ Bald eagles are in fact completely bald.

2. _____ The sheaf of arrows on the Great Seal probably signifies our country's willingness to defend itself.

3. _____ The olive branch on the Great Seal probably signifies that the United States is a peace-loving nation.

4. _____ Words like *wingspread* and *shoreline* are called compound words.

5. _____ In the United States today, the bald eagle's habitat is threatened by conservationists.

6. _____ Male bald eagles are quite a bit larger than females.

7. _____ According to the U.S. Fish and Wildlife Service, all raptors are on the brink of extinction.

VOCABULARY

Circle a letter to show the meaning of the **boldface** word or words.

1. The eagle's decline was **attributed** to loss of prey and habitat.

     a. named as the source of   b. praised and commended for   c. deliberately sabotaged by

2. **Real estate** development threatens the eagle's future.

   a. actual rather than fictional

   b. huge mansions and estates

   c. land and anything on it

3. The truth of his **contention** was obvious; where the shoreline was crowded with people, there were no eagles.

   a. stated opinion

   b. very hard to believe

   c. longingly hoped for outcome

4. Bald eagles were on the **brink** of extinction.

   a. too few to be counted

   b. the point just short of

   c. stranded in unhealthy places

5. In the lower 48 states, there were fewer than 500 **breeding pairs** of eagles.

   a. married couples who bred eagles

   b. male and female eagles who produce offspring

   c. purebred eagles

6. A **pesticide** called DDT caused female eagles to lay brittle eggs.

   a. insect or animal that destroys crops

   b. deadly, infectious disease

   c. poison used to kill insects, weeds, etc.

ANTONYMS

Unscramble the words from the reading. Then write each unscrambled word next to its *antonym* (word with the opposite meaning).

SHAVIN _____   SKINHRS _____

TRIBELT _____   NEDNAB _____

GARLE _____   ACOERUG _____

1. cowardice _____   4. expands _____

2. soft _____   5. small _____

3. allowed _____   6. appear _____

PENGUINS AT RISK

Before reading . . .

A sunken freighter is a big financial loss to a shipping company. But the damage to nature can be much greater. This lesson recounts the African penguin's narrow escape from a recent oil spill.

Mammoth Rescue Effort Saves 10,000 Vulnerable Seabirds

Hundreds of volunteers flocked to Cape Town, South Africa, when they heard the news. A fuel spill from a sunken freighter had created a 12-square-mile oil slick. The main breeding ground of the African penguins was completely surrounded!

Conservationists say it was the largest rescue effort ever. The notorious *Exxon Valdez* oil spill in Alaska was certainly larger. But rescuers there were able to save only 1,500 birds—less than a tenth of the number that were cleaned up in Cape Town.

Saving the penguins is hard work. Using detergent and toothbrushes, it takes two people an hour to clean up each bird. And the birds had to be hand-fed sardines—or they would starve. Most required more than a month of care before they regained enough strength to be released.

Most of the contaminated birds were rescued from Robben Island. This island off the southern tip of Africa is home to the third largest breeding colony of African penguins. In all, more than two-fifths of the 150,000 African penguins were threatened by the oil spill.

Rescuers were determined to prevent annihilation of the species. So they accomplished what was said to be "the biggest attempted movement of birds in the world." They actually put 10,000 birds in boxes and drove them 560 miles east. There, in

Most of the world's penguins live near Antarctica, around the South Pole. African penguins—which are about 18 inches tall and weigh about seven pounds—are one of the few species that breed farther north.

18

the mainland town of Port Elizabeth, the birds were released into the sea. Authorities said it took them about 11 days to swim home—which was time enough for most of the oil to dissipate.

Have you ever seen a penguin? Many people say that penguins look like fat little men in dress suits. On land, these birds stand up straight on short legs and walk with a clumsy waddle. Their backs are black, and their breasts are white. The males and females look almost alike. They have short flipper-like wings that look like arms from a distance. Because their legs are far back on their bodies, they are poor runners. Some penguins slide on land. They fall forward and shove themselves with their feet, like paddlewheel steamboats! Penguins defend themselves with their beaks. Their eyes are very sensitive to light.

FASCINATING FACTS

- The largest penguin, the *emperor*, is about three and one-half feet tall.

- Penguins can often be seen taking rides on moving ice floes—just for fun!

- Some penguins have "sticky fingers." They steal pebbles that other penguins have gathered to build their nests. As they set off to steal a pebble, they slink along quietly.

- Scientists say that penguins lost their ability to fly millions of years ago.

Penguins are protected from cold water by their feathers, which secrete an oil. They also have a layer of fat under the skin. Their wings have a scaly covering, and the wing bones are flattened to make better paddles. The breast plumage is soft and silvery. Furriers once used these feathers to make muffs and collars.

Penguins are most at home in the water. They are wonderful swimmers and divers, and can catch fish underwater with great ease. They can stay underwater for 45 seconds or longer. Some have been known to swim at a speed of 20 miles an hour. They use their wings as paddles when they swim. Penguins spend most of their time in the water. But nearly all of them return to land to breed and raise their young.

On land, penguins live in colonies. They are so crowded in their nesting places that they barely leave room for the nests. Some penguins keep the same mates for many years. They also may keep the same nesting place. The nests are often made of sticks, stones, and grass. They may be out in the open, or they may be hidden in a crevice.

The male penguin usually helps to care for the young, which are helpless for many weeks. However, as soon as the young can walk, they join groups of other youngsters. These babies huddle together to keep warm and are watched over by a few adults. The other adults hunt food.

COMPREHENSION

Circle the word or words that correctly complete each sentence.

1. Most of the world's penguins live near the (North / South) Pole.

2. Cleaning up contaminated birds can only be done by (hand / machine).

3. Penguins' breeding grounds are very (lonely / crowded) places.

4. The fastest penguins can swim (40 / 20) miles per hour.

5. (More / Fewer) birds were saved in Africa than in Alaska.

6. On land, penguins get around by (waddling and sliding / paddling and diving).

SENTENCE COMPLETION

Unscramble the words from the reading to correctly complete the sentences.

1. Penguins' backs are **CKABL** _____, and their breasts are **THEWI** _____.

2. Penguins are most at home in the **EWART** _____.

3. **TENGDREET** _____ is used to clean contaminated birds.

4. African penguins do not **DEBER** _____ in Antarctica.

5. Some penguins keep the same **STEAM** _____ for many years.

6. Port Elizabeth is **TAES** _____ of Robben Island.

CRITICAL THINKING

What is the main difference between penguins and most other birds?

_____

PUZZLER

Use the clues to help you solve the crossword puzzle. Answers are words that complete the sentences.

ACROSS

2. A penguin's _____ have a scaly covering.

5. Penguins catch fish with great _____.

8. Rescuers hand-fed the penguins _____.

9. Hundreds of _____ rushed to Cape Town to help save the penguins.

10. Penguins like to take rides on ice _____.

DOWN

1. An _____ slick occurs after a fuel spill.

3. Penguins' eyes are _____ to light.

4. About 10,000 penguins were _____ in Cape Town.

6. The _____ is the largest penguin.

7. Nests may be hidden in a _____.

SYLLABLES

Divide the words from the reading into *syllables* (separate sounds).

| authorities | Antarctica | annihilation |

1. _____ / _____ / _____ / _____

_____ / _____ / _____ / _____

2. _____ / _____ / _____ / _____ / _____

VOCABULARY

Circle a letter to show the meaning of the **boldface** word or words.

1. When they heard about the oil spill, hundreds of volunteers **flocked** to Cape Town.

   a. flew together   b. came to   c. made travel plans

2. Alaska's **notorious** *Exxon Valdez* oil spill extended over a huge area.

   a. widely known   b. famous as a   c. noted in newspapers
        as a bad thing   good example   around the world

3. When on land, penguins live in **colonies**.

   a. social   b. ice structures   c. groups of people
        organizations   with many   or animals living
        like clubs   rooms   near each other

4. **Furriers** once used penguin feathers to make soft collars.

   a. people who collect   b. those who make garments   c. old-time
        fur from animals   from animal hides   trappers

WORD COMPLETION

Add vowels (*a, e, i, o, u*) to complete the words from the reading.

1. A C R__V__C__ is a crack or narrow opening in a wall of earth or rock.

2. P L__M__G__ is another name for a bird's feathers.

3. The __N N__H__L__T__ __N of something is its complete destruction.

4. A F R__ __G H T__R is a ship that transports cargo from one place to another.

5. Those who S T__ __L are sometimes said to have "sticky fingers."

6. A penguin's short wings could be called F L__P P__R-L__K__.

COMPOUND WORDS

Write a *compound word* (one word made by combining two or more words) from the reading to answer each question.

1. What were used as tools to clean the contaminated birds? _____

2. What do penguins look like when they lie on their stomachs and move ahead by using their feet like paddlewheels? _____

3. Where is Port Elizabeth located? _____

ANTONYMS

Draw a line connecting each **boldface** word from the reading with its *antonym* (word that means the opposite).

1. **contaminated**   a. intensify

2. **dissipate**   b. purified

3. **secrete**   c. protected

4. **slink**   d. difficulty

5. **threatened**   e. absorb

6. **ease**   f. strut

RECALLING DETAILS

Use information from the reading to answer the questions.

1. What did the volunteers feed the rescued penguins? _____

2. Where is Robben Island located? _____

   _____

3. What body part does a penguin use to defend itself? _____

4. How long does it take to clean up a contaminated penguin? _____

THE GREAT WHITE SHARK

Before reading . . .

Great white sharks are large-brained, highly intelligent creatures. But their bloodthirsty image has often been used to justify slaughter. Every year, many great whites are killed. Attitudes are changing, however. The species is now protected in California and South Africa.

The streamlined body of the great white shark makes it one of the fastest—and most dangerous—fish in the sea. The great white is the largest of all predatory sharks. It can reach a length of more than 20 feet and weigh more than 7,000 pounds.

The great white shark is one of the most efficient predators on earth. It can locate its prey with astounding accuracy and kill it with a single, devastating bite. It is the only shark that regularly attacks warmblooded animals, such as seals and dolphins. Its diet also includes squid, sea turtles, seabirds, and whale carcasses. Experts say that great whites are always hungry. No matter how much they eat, they are never satisfied.

The great white's teeth are broad, sharp, and serrated like steak knives. On a scale of hardness, their teeth rank with steel. When they do get worn out, they shear off cleanly. Then sharp new teeth move up from behind to replace them.

A great white can hear sounds from a mile away. Through small pores in its snout, it can pick up electrical nerve signals in its prey. Other sensors can detect blood in the water. The great white is also well-equipped to see in the dim underwater light. Just before an

In spite of their bad reputation, great white sharks rarely attack people. Each year, three times as many people are killed by lightning as are killed by sharks. And 100 more people die from bee stings each year than from shark bites. Most human victims of shark attacks survive. According to scientists, this suggests that the great white dislikes human flesh.

attack, its big black eyes roll back into their sockets for protection. And a hungry shark often pokes its head out of the water. Why? To sniff the air for scent of prey.

The great white shark never gets sick. It has mysterious antibodies that make it immune to practically every known bacterial invader. It is also one of the few animals known to be completely immune to cancer.

The great white shark roams at large in many of the world's seas and oceans. It is mainly found off the coasts of North America, Australia, southern Africa, New Zealand, Japan, and parts of the Mediterranean. It spends most of its time around reefs—where there are plenty of fish and sea mammals.

The great white prefers temperate water. It is very rare in polar and tropical regions. It has been known, however, to sometimes wander as far north as Alaska.

Great whites never stop swimming. They swim at a slow pace, without wasting energy. One reason for this is that their prey is often widely scattered. Sometimes great whites go without food for weeks or even months. They must keep moving in search of prey. They also need to keep swimming to force oxygenated water through their gills.

The female great white gives birth in an unusual way. Unlike most fish, she doesn't cast countless eggs into the water. She gives birth to a few fully formed young. Newborn great whites are completely independent. In a sense, however, the mother looks after them *before* they are born. She does this by only giving birth in the shallows—where her young are less likely to become another shark's meal.

The great white shark is the only animal in the sea with no natural enemies. Even killer whales normally avoid this dangerous predator.

COMPREHENSION

Write **T** or **F** to show whether each statement is *true* or *false.* Write **NI** if there is *no information* in the reading to help you make a judgment.

1. _____ Human beings rarely survive attack by a great white shark.

2. _____ A great white shark weighs a little more than two African elephants.

3. _____ The female great white produces offspring in the same way that all fish do.

4. _____ Because great whites are always hungry, they can never stop swimming.

5. _____ You wouldn't be likely to find a great white shark near the South Pole.

6. _____ Unlike fish, seals and dolphins are warmblooded animals.

SUFFIXES

Rewrite the **boldface** word to complete each sentence. Add a suffix from the box to make the correct word form. Hint: You will *not* use all the suffixes in the box.

-ies	-ated	-er	-ity	-est	-ious	-al	-less

1. The great white is the **(large)** _____ of all predatory sharks.

2. The shark can pick up **(electric)** _____ nerve signals in its prey.

3. Constant swimming forces **(oxygen)** _____ water through the shark's gills.

4. The shark's **(mystery)** _____ antibodies make it immune to disease.

5. Most fish cast **(count)** _____ eggs into the water.

PUZZLER

Use the clues to help you solve the crossword puzzle. Answers are words that complete the sentences.

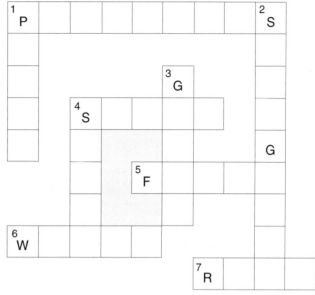

ACROSS

1. The great white is one of the world's most efficient _____.

4. Its diet includes seals, dolphins, and _____.

5. The great white seems to dislike human _____.

6. It prefers temperate _____.

7. Shark attacks on people are _____.

DOWN

1. A shark sometimes _____ its head out of the water.

2. The shark's bloodthirsty image has been used to justify its _____.

3. Oxygenated water is taken in through the shark's _____.

4. Pores in the shark's _____ act as sensors.

ALPHABETICAL ORDER

List the words from the reading in alphabetical order.

pace	accuracy	shallows	efficient	astounding
scents	sensor	invader	immune	sockets

1. _____

2. _____

3. _____

4. _____

5. _____

6. _____

7. _____

8. _____

9. _____

10. _____

VOCABULARY

Circle a letter to show the meaning of the **boldface** word or words.

1. The great white shark is **immune** to practically every known disease.

   a. protected against   b. vulnerable to   c. vaccinated for

2. For protection, the shark's eyes can roll back into their **sockets**.

   a. short, stocking-   b. combination eyelids   c. hollow parts into
   like fin coverings   and eyelashes   which things fit

3. The great white spends most of its time around **reefs**.

   a. islands just   b. ridges of coral   c. long beds
   off the   or rock near   of kelp and
   shoreline   the surface   seaweed

4. On a scale of hardness, the great white's teeth **rank with** steel.

   a. compare very   b. have an unpleasant   c. weigh a great
   closely to   smell and taste   deal more than

5. The great white's worn-out teeth **shear off** cleanly.

   a. become whiter   b. sharpen themselves   c. break away

6. The great white's teeth are **serrated** like steak knives.

   a. lined up in a   b. extremely sharp   c. edged with
   straight row   and pointed   sawlike notches

SYLLABLES

Divide the words from the reading into *syllables* (separate sounds).

attitudes	independent	efficient	reputation

1. _____ / _____ / _____   _____ / _____ / _____

2. _____ / _____ / _____ / _____

   _____ / _____ / _____ / _____

28

ANTONYMS

First, unscramble the words from the reading to complete the sentences. Then select *antonyms* (words that mean the opposite) from the box. Write the antonyms on the lines. Hint: You will *not* use all the words in the box.

remarkable	unremarkable	perish	brilliant
fictional	conservation	polar	blurry
dangerous	lukewarm	frigid	wasteful

ANTONYM

1. The great white shark is one of the most
   FICEITENF _____ predators.   _____

2. The great white prefers **EPRATMEET**
   _____ waters.   _____

3. It can see well in the **MID** _____
   underwater light.   _____

4. The great white's bad reputation has been used
   to justify its **LAUGHTERS** _____. _____

5. The shark can locate its prey with
   DOGUNSTAIN _____ accuracy. _____

6. Most human victims of shark attacks
   VIRUSEV _____.   _____

SPELLING

Circle the correctly spelled word in each group.

1. carrcases   carcasses   carcases

2. intelligent   intellagent   intelligant

3. devestating   devistating   devastating

4. practicaly   practiccaly   practically

IDENTIFYING ANIMALS

Complete each sentence with one of the following animal names: *grizzly bear, bald eagle, African penguins, great white shark.*

1. On land, _____ live in colonies.

2. The _____ has a slow reproductive cycle.

3. A _____ is pictured on the Great Seal of the United States.

4. A _____ must keep moving in search of prey.

FACT OR OPINION?

Write **F** or **O** to show whether each statement is a *fact* or an *opinion.*

1. _____ The great white shark is the only sea animal with no natural enemies.

2. _____ To protect the bald eagle, real estate development along the Potomac should be stopped immediately.

3. _____ Idaho ranchers who block the grizzly's return care nothing about the ecosystem.

4. _____ Penguins are poor runners, but they are excellent swimmers and divers.

5. _____ Human swimmers actually have little to fear from great white sharks.

6. _____ The U.S. Fish and Wildlife Service wants to remove the bald eagle from its endangered species list.

SPORTS SPECTACULARS

LESSON 1: The Immortal Babe Ruth

LESSON 2: The History of Tennis

LESSON 3: The Olympics

LESSON 4: The Iditarod

When you complete this unit, you will be able to answer questions like these:

■ *At the beginning of Babe Ruth's career, what team did he play for?*

■ *Who was the first professional tennis player? How much was she paid for a tour?*

■ *What Olympic race was first run 2,500 years ago?*

■ *How many miles must a dogsled cover to complete the famous race called the Iditarod?*

PRETEST

Write **T** or **F** to show whether you think each statement is *true* or *false*.

1. _____ Siberian huskies are one of the most popular breeds to be trained as sled dogs.

2. _____ The Olympic Games are named after the town of Olympia, Washington.

3. _____ Babe Ruth set a record for most innings pitched in a World Series game.

4. _____ Wimbledon, England, is the site of the world's first tennis game.

5. _____ The Olympic Games are organized as an official athletic competition among nations.

6. _____ A dogsled driver yells commands to the lead dogs.

Pretest answers: 1. T 2. F 3. T 4. F 5. F 6. T

THE IMMORTAL BABE RUTH

Before reading . . .

This lesson capsulizes Babe Ruth's amazing baseball career. The three stories are taken from the sports pages of hometown newspapers. Notice the different datelines that lead off the articles.

Babe on the Mound

BOSTON, Mass., Oct. 9, 1916—Boston pitcher George Herman "Babe" Ruth got off to a rocky start today. Fans were nervous when he gave up a first-inning home run to Brooklyn's Hi Myers. But by the time the 14-inning game was over, Ruth had held Brooklyn to only six hits. With today's 2–1 triumph, Boston took a 2–0 lead in the World Series. In going the distance, Ruth set a record for most innings pitched in a World Series game.

Ruth struck out three and walked three as Brooklyn left five men on base. This was the first Series victory for the young lefthander. During the regular season, he compiled an impressive 23–12 record, including nine shutouts. His earned-run average was 1.75—a record low for a lefthanded pitcher.

A Ruthian Feat

ST. LOUIS, Mo., Oct. 9, 1928—The Babe didn't seem to notice the boos, hisses, jeers—or the bottles thrown from the left-field stands. Instead, he continued his torrid hitting streak today by swatting three home runs, leading the New York Yankees to a 7–3 World Series victory over St. Louis.

As the Yankees swept all four games of the Series, Ruth's 10 hits in 16 times at bat gave him a record .625 batting average. Lou Gehrig, who also clouted a circuit blast today, had four round-trippers in the Series, tying the Babe's 1926 mark.

Ruth played the entire Series with a bum knee. But the injury didn't prevent him from making a spectacular one-handed, knee-sliding grab of a fly ball to end the game and the Series. With that, the jeering Cardinal fans were silenced at last.

The Bambino Bows Out

BOSTON, Mass., June 2, 1935—Marking the end of an era, Babe Ruth was released from the Boston Braves today. According to manager Bill McKechnie, the decision was made because Ruth violated curfew regulations. But the 41-year-old legend had been nothing more than a drawing card for the hapless Braves, wallowing in the National League cellar.

A chronic knee injury had sharply reduced the Bambino's playing time. In his last game on May 30, he played left field only briefly and failed to get a hit in his one time at bat.

But only a week ago, Ruth showed he was still capable of destroying pitchers. At Forbes Field in Pittsburgh, the Babe smashed three home runs off Pirate hurlers. They were the 712th, 713th, and 714th home runs of his career—which began as a lefthanded pitcher with the Boston Red Sox in 1914.

The Sultan of Swat started out in Baltimore. There, as a seven-year-old street urchin, he was sent to St. Mary's Industrial Home. Although he went on to earn international respect and admiration, he never lost the rough edge of his origins.

Harry Hooper, an early Boston teammate, had this tribute: "Sometimes I still can't believe what I saw—this 19-year-old kid, crude, poorly educated . . . gradually transformed into the idol of American youth and the symbol of baseball the world over."

COMPREHENSION

Write **T** or **F** if the statement is *true* or *false*. Write **NI** if there is *no information* in the reading to help you make a judgment.

1. _____ Babe Ruth's baseball career ended in the same city where it began.

2. _____ Babe pitched lefthanded, but he batted righthanded.

3. _____ During the regular season in 1916, Babe's pitching record was 22–13.

4. _____ By 1935, Babe Ruth had lost his amazing ability to hit home runs.

5. _____ Babe's professional baseball career extended from 1914 to 1935.

6. _____ In 1935, the Detroit Tigers won the World Series.

FIGURATIVE LANGUAGE

Circle a letter to show the meaning of each **boldface** word or phrase. Use context clues to help you figure out the definitions.

1. In **going the distance**, Ruth set a record for the most innings pitched in a World Series game.

   a. not giving up a single hit
   b. pitching the whole game
   c. traveling the farthest to get there

2. Ruth never lost the **rough edge of his origins**.

   a. bumpy skin he had inherited
   b. harsh way of dealing with people
   c. undisciplined behavior of his boyhood

3. Babe had been nothing more than a **drawing card** for the Braves.

   a. attraction to lure fans
   b. talented illustrator
   c. worn-out has-been

4. Ruth was accused of violating **curfew regulations**.

   a. rules against   b. registering   c. making others
       staying out   for the team   break curfew
       too late   curfew   rules

5. In the 1928 World Series, Lou Gehrig hit four **round-trippers**.

   a. visiting   b. doubles and   c. home
       fans   triples   runs

PUZZLER

Use the clues to help you solve the crossword puzzle. Answers are words that complete the sentences.

ACROSS

1. During the course of his career, Ruth earned international _____.

3. Babe played with an _____ during the 1928 World Series.

6. Boston defeated _____ in the 1916 World Series.

7. The Babe's real name was _____ Herman Ruth.

DOWN

2. The _____ were defeated in the 1928 World Series.

4. Babe Ruth and Lou Gehrig played for the New York _____.

5. Babe's batting _____ for the 1928 Series was .625.

6. Babe was a pitcher when he played ball in _____.

COMPOUND WORDS

Write *compound words* (one word that combines two or more words) to complete the sentences. For each compound, choose the first part from Box A and the second part from Box B. Hint: You will *not* use all the words.

┌─ BOX A ─┐			
date	shut	news	left
right	team	home	put

┌─ BOX B ─┐			
paper	town	outs	field
line	hander	team	mate

1. The young _____ won his first Series victory on October 9, 1916.

2. During the regular season in 1916, Ruth pitched nine

   _____ .

3. Harry Hooper had been a _____ of the Babe's in Boston.

4. The sports stories in this lesson first appeared in

   _____ newspapers.

5. The _____ on each story tells when and where the event happened.

6. According to the _____ article, Babe hit his 714th homer in Pittsburgh.

NOTING DETAILS

Circle the word from the reading that correctly completes each sentence.

1. An injury to Babe's (elbow / knee) gave him trouble through the years.

2. One of Babe Ruth's nicknames was "the (Sultan / Samson) of Swat."

3. Ruth spent his youth at St. Mary's Industrial Home in (Baltimore / Boston).

4. Babe made a spectacular (hit / catch) to end the 1928 World Series.

VOCABULARY

First, unscramble the words from the reading. Each word is a *synonym* (word that means the same) of one of the **boldface** words in the sentences. Write the correct synonym (unscrambled word) on the line after each sentence.

PURMHIT _____   SHAPELS _____

HUNRIC _____   RUSHLER _____

RIDROT _____   LOID _____

1. The Babe smashed three home runs off Pirate **pitchers**.   _____

2. With today's 2–1 **victory**, Boston took a 2–0 lead in the World Series.   _____

3. Before going to St. Mary's, George Herman Ruth was a **mischievous boy** on the streets of Baltimore.   _____

4. The Boston Braves were an **unfortunate** team in 1935.   _____

5. Over the years of his career, Babe became the **hero** of American youth.   _____

6. The Babe's **hot** hitting streak continued on October 9, 1928.   _____

DRAWING CONCLUSIONS

Reread the article entitled "A Ruthian Feat." Then explain why you think the St. Louis fans booed and hissed at Babe Ruth. Write in complete sentences.

_____

_____

_____

THE HISTORY OF TENNIS

Before reading . . .

Anyone for a game of *sphairistike*? In 1873, British Major Walter Wingfield introduced this new game. Although the name was unpopular and disappeared almost immediately, the game itself spread rapidly. But both players and spectators had started calling the new game "lawn tennis."

900 Years Ago

An ancient form of tennis was actually played as early as the 12th century. There were no rackets then. Players hit the ball with the palms of their hands. The ball was made of pieces of cloth bunched and sewn in a round shape. Needless to say, it didn't bounce very well! The "net" was either a rope or a pile of dirt.

In Major Wingfield's version of the old game, players used a plain rubber ball and a spoon-shaped racket. And the game was played on a grass court shaped like an hourglass.

Tennis came to the United States via Bermuda. It was there, in 1874, that a young American woman named Mary Outerbridge watched British soldiers playing lawn tennis. She convinced them to let her play, too, and she loved it. Mary bought some equipment and took it home. Then she and her brother built a court on Staten Island, New York.

The game caught on quickly. In 1881, the U.S. Lawn Tennis Association was formed. That same year the first national championship games were held at Newport, Rhode Island.

TENNIS TRIVIA

About 100 years ago, rules for tennis clothing were very strict. Men wore long pants, and women wore long skirts, long-sleeved blouses, and sometimes even hats! In 1905, May Sutton, a 17-year-old American, was in a women's singles match at Wimbledon. One player complained about May's outfit. Why? Because a little bit of her ankles could be seen, and she was wearing a short-sleeved blouse. She was ordered to lower the hem on her dress before the match went on. May won the match.

Professional Tennis

A shocking thing happened in 1926. French tennis star Susanne Lenglen was paid $50,000 for a tour! That was how professional tennis got its start. Today, it is hard to imagine the uproar this caused among uppercrust tennis buffs. They thought it was "vulgar" to play a game for money. It wasn't until 1968 that professionals were allowed to play at the annual tournament at Wimbledon. Now, most amateur champions become pros after several years of amateur competition.

Perhaps the most colorful and popular tennis tournament in the world is held each July at Wimbledon, England. The best players from all over the world come to compete there.

The first Wimbledon was held in 1877, when only 22 players—none of them women— took part in the games. There was only one prize, and only 200 fans came out to watch. They were all dressed up and behaved very properly. There were no stands for the spectators to sit in, so they sat on the ground or in their horse-drawn carriages.

In the finals, Spencer William Gore played William Marshall. At that time the overhead serve was not in use. Both men served the ball in a side-arm style. Throughout the match, Gore kept reaching over the net to hit the ball. This made the judges angry—but there was no rule against it. In the end, Gore was the winner. "Lawn tennis is a bit boring," he said. "It will never catch on." How wrong he was!

THE LONGEST VOLLEY

In tennis, a *volley* is a return of the ball before it hits the ground. On January 7, 1936, two tennis players volleyed for 78 straight minutes! They were Helen Wills Moody and Howard Kinsey. They hit the ball 2,001 times without stopping. Perhaps they could have volleyed even longer. They quit because Kinsey had to leave for a tennis lesson.

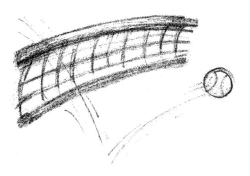

COMPREHENSION

Write **T** or **F** if the statement is *true* or *false.* Write **NI** if there is *no information* to help you make a judgment.

1. _____ British soldiers in Bermuda invented the modern form of tennis.

2. _____ Martina Navratilova has earned more money than any other woman in professional tennis.

3. _____ Twenty-two players took part in the first tournament at Wimbledon.

4. _____ In 1905, some people were shocked to see a female tennis player's bare arms.

5. _____ A man named Major Outerbridge introduced the modern game of tennis.

6. _____ In the ancient form of tennis, players struck a cloth ball with their knees and elbows.

SPELLING

Circle the correctly spelled word in each group.

1. annaul   annual   anuall

2. amateur   amatuer   amachure

3. vulgar   vulger   vulgir

SYLLABLES

Divide the words from the reading into *syllables* (separate sounds).

Wimbledon	**Bermuda**	**tournament**	**spectators**

_____ / _____ / _____   _____ / _____ / _____

_____ / _____ / _____   _____ / _____ / _____

PUZZLER

Use the clues to help you solve the crossword puzzle. Answers are words that complete the sentences.

ACROSS

1. A spectator at a tennis match is called a _____.

5. In 1881, a _____ was held in Newport, R.I.

6. One player complained that May Sutton's _____ were showing.

9. To hit a _____, return the ball before it hits the ground.

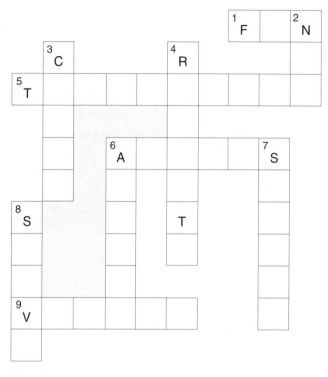

DOWN

2. The first tennis _____ was a rope or a dirt pile.

3. *Sphairistike* was played on a grass _____.

4. The first _____ were spoon-shaped.

6. An _____ tournament is held at Wimbledon.

7. There were no _____ at the first Wimbledon tournament.

8. The overhead _____ was not used by Gore or Marshall.

SENTENCE COMPLETION

Unscramble the *adjectives* (words that describe nouns or pronouns) from the reading to complete each sentence.

1. The **RANGY** _____ judges could not stop Spencer Gore from reaching over the net.

2. The **STEB** _____ players from all over the world play at Wimbledon.

3. A 17-year-old American was playing a **LESSING** _____ match at Wimbledon.

4. Two tennis players volleyed for 78 **GITHSTAR** _____ minutes.

5. The game called *sphairistike* was soon renamed **N A W L** _____ tennis.

SYNONYMS AND ANTONYMS

Find a *synonym* (word that means the same) or an *antonym* (word that means the opposite) for each **boldface** word in the sentences. Write it on the line.
Hint: You will *not* use all the words in the box.

fascinating	permitted	struck	served	politely
disbanded	commanded	vulgar	winner	amateurs

1. In 1968, **professionals** were allowed to play at Wimbledon for the first time.   ANTONYM: _____

2. Spectators at the first Wimbledon tournament behaved very **properly**.   SYNONYM: _____

3. May Sutton was **ordered** to lower the hem on her dress.   SYNONYM: _____

4. William Marshall was the **loser** of the first finals match played at Wimbledon.   ANTONYM: _____

5. Helen Moody and Howard Kinsey **hit** the ball 2,001 times without stopping.   SYNONYM: _____

6. The U.S. Lawn Tennis Association was **formed** in 1881.   ANTONYM: _____

7. Women were not **allowed** to play in the first tournament at Wimbledon.   SYNONYM: _____

8. Spencer William Gore thought lawn tennis was a bit **boring**.   ANTONYM: _____

VOCABULARY

Circle a letter to show the meaning of the **boldface** word or words.

1. Suzanne Lenglen was paid $50,000 for a tennis **tour**.

   a. sightseeing
      visit to France
   b. giving several radio
      and TV interviews
   c. playing tennis in
      several different cities

2. Members of the **upper crust** objected to the very idea of professional tennis.

   a. snobbish
      high society
   b. top-ranked
      amateur players
   c. crusty old
      sportswriters

3. They thought it was **vulgar** to play a game for money.

   a. dangerously
      vulnerable
   b. conceited;
      boastful
   c. distastefully
      lower class

4. In 1926, tennis **buffs** had different ideas than they do now.

   a. expert players
   b. enthusiastic fans
   c. official rule-makers

5. In Major Wingfield's **version** of the old game, players used spoon-shaped rackets.

   a. particular
      variation
   b. handwritten
      rulebook
   c. unpopular
      name

SUFFIXES

Rewrite the **boldface** words, adding the *suffix* used in the reading.

1. The U.S. Lawn Tennis **(Associate)** _____ began in 1881.

2. Mary brought tennis **(equip)** _____ home from Bermuda.

3. At first, **(profession)** _____ tennis caused an uproar.

4. The annual tournament at Wimbledon is popular and **(color)** _____.

THE OLYMPICS

Before reading . . .

Every four years, millions of people around the world look forward to watching the Olympic Games on TV. Did you know that the first Olympics had only one event—and that it was held 2,750 years ago?

Every four years, athletes from nations throughout the world compete in the Olympic Games. No other sports spectacle has a background so historic or thrilling.

Opening Ceremonies

Flags flutter from the top of a crowd-filled stadium. Cheers ring out as a runner enters the arena carrying a blazing torch to light the Olympic flame. The lighted torch has been brought many miles from Greece, where the games began so long ago. The athletes march into the stadium behind their national flags. They stand at attention and promise to obey the rules of sportsmanship and fair play. The host nation then proclaims the opening of the Olympic Games.

Competing for Honor and Glory

The purpose of the Olympic Games is to let the great athletes of the world vie with each other in a spirit of peace and friendship. Olympic athletes pledge to respect the regulations that govern them. They agree to participate for the honor of their country and for the glory of sports. Nations do not actually compete against each other. Sportswriters credit countries with points in events between teams or individuals. But this practice of ranking nation against nation is entirely unofficial. No nation ever officially "wins" the Olympics.

Winners of Olympic events receive gold medals. Second-place winners receive silver medals. Bronze medals go to third-place winners. The fourth-, fifth-, and sixth-place athletes receive certificates.

THE OLYMPIC MOTTO

The official motto of the Olympics is (in Latin) *Citius, Altius, Fortius*. These words mean "swifter, higher, stronger."

Two Seasons, Two Locations

Olympic events are divided into summer and winter games. The Summer Olympics run for about two weeks, and the Winter Olympics last 10 days. The official flag of the Olympic Games is white with five interlocking rings of blue, yellow, black, red, and green at its center. At least one of those colors appears in the national flag of every country.

Olympic "Firsts"

- In the little town of Olympia, Greece, the first recorded "Olympic" race was held in 776 B.C.

- Jumping, discus throwing, wrestling, and javelin throwing were added to the Olympic races about 708 B.C.

- The ruins of the ancient Olympic stadium in Athens were excavated in 1878.

- The first modern Olympics was held in 1896.

- Women athletes first appeared in the Olympics in 1900.

- In 1920, the Olympic flag was used for the first time.

- Winter games were first added to the Olympics in 1924.

The Longest "Timeout"— 1,500 Years!

The noble purpose of the Olympic Games gradually declined along with the Greek city-states. About 60 A.D., the Emperor Nero entered the games as a contestant. Nero was a poor athlete. By competing, he lowered the Olympic standards of sportsmanship and athletic skill. The games became so corrupt that Emperor Theodisius abolished them in 394 A.D. More than 1,500 years passed before a Frenchman organized a renewal of the Olympic Games.

THE MARATHON

The longest race in the Olympic Games is the *marathon*. Over the years, that word has become a synonym for any long-term test of endurance. But the original Marathon was really a *place*—a small village in ancient Greece. The race was named to honor a young man who ran from Marathon to Athens in 490 B.C. He was a messenger carrying news of victory in a great battle fought between the Athenians and the Persians.

This victory was important because it saved Athens. As the story goes, the messenger fell dead from exhaustion once his news was delivered. Inspired by the messenger's feat, the Greeks went on to defeat the Persians once and for all. If you visited Marathon today, you could still see the mound that was raised over the Athenians who fell in battle. The Olympic event called the *marathon* is a race over an open course of precisely 26 miles, 385 yards—supposedly the exact distance between Marathon and Athens.

For your information: In 1896, the winning male marathoner ran the race in two hours and 58 minutes. In 1996, the winning runner finished the race in two hours and 12 minutes.

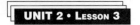

COMPREHENSION

Circle the word or words that correctly complete each sentence.

1. In the Olympics, nations (do / do not) officially compete against one another.

2. The Olympic flag has (eight / five) interlocking rings of different colors.

3. The Olympic Games are held every (six / four) years.

4. A messenger carried war news from Marathon to Athens about (3,500 / 2,500) years ago.

5. In 1920, the Olympic (flag / torch) was used for the first time.

6. In 490 B.C., the Athenians were at war with the (Spartans / Persians).

ANTONYMS

Find the incorrect word in each sentence and cross it out. Then find the correct word (the *antonym* of the crossed-out word) in the box and write it on the line. Hint: You will *not* use all the words in the box.

interesting	victory	poor	excavated	noble
abolished	admired	corrupt	questionable	rebuilt

1. Emperor Theodisius started the Olympic Games in 394 A.D. _____

2. In Athens, the ancient Olympic stadium was buried in 1878. _____

3. The shameful purpose of the Olympic games gradually declined. _____

4. The Emperor Nero was an outstanding athlete. _____

5. When the Olympic standards for sportsmanship were lowered, the games became pure.

   _____

6. A messenger carried news of defeat to the Athenians.

   _____

PUZZLER

Use the clues to help you solve the crossword puzzle. Answers are words that complete the sentences.

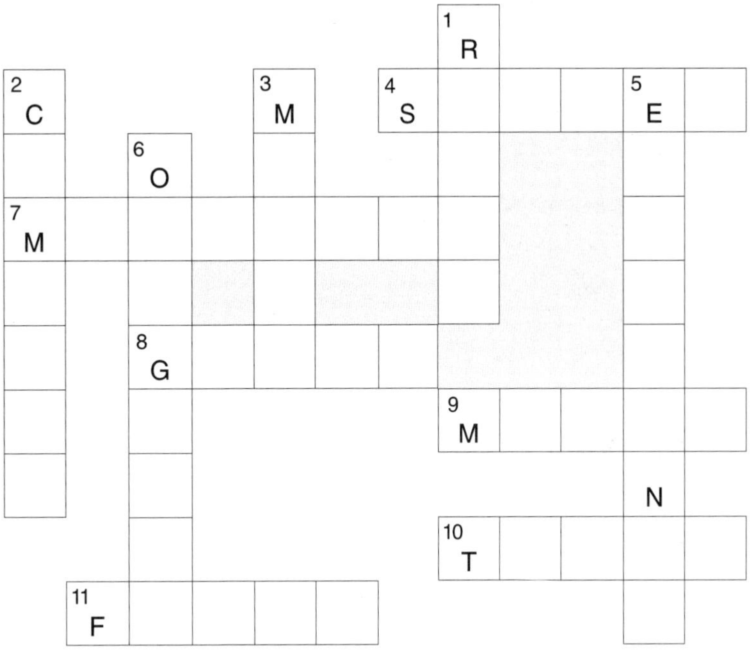

ACROSS

4. Olympic events are divided into the _____ games and the winter games.

7. A messenger carried war news from _____ to Athens.

8. Athletes compete for the _____ of sports.

9. A winner of an Olympic event receives a gold _____.

10. A runner carries a blazing _____ into the arena.

11. Cheers ring out as the Olympic _____ is lighted.

DOWN

1. The _____ of the ancient Olympic stadium were found in Athens.

2. Athletes from many nations _____ in Olympic events.

3. The _____ of the Olympics is "Citius, altius, fortius."

5. Any long-term test of _____ is often called a marathon.

6. The _____ Marathon was a small village.

Crossword grid clues (letter positions):
- 1 Down: R
- 2 Down: C
- 3 Down: M
- 4 Across: S
- 5 Down: E
- 6 Down: O
- 7 Across: M
- 8 Across: G
- 9 Across: M
- 10 Across: T
- 11 Across: F
- N

NOTING DETAILS

Use information from the reading to help you answer the questions.

1. In order to complete the race, what distance must a marathoner run? _____

2. An athlete who finishes a race in second place wins what kind of medal? _____

3. In what year did female athletes first participate in Olympic events? _____

VOCABULARY

Circle a letter to show the meaning of each **boldface** word.

1. The great athletes of the world **vie** with each other in the spirit of friendship.

   a. socialize   b. compete   c. cooperate

2. Olympic athletes **pledge** to respect the regulations that govern them.

   a. force   b. pawn   c. promise

3. The official **motto** of the Olympics was originally written in Latin.

   a. statement of a   b. trademark   c. logo for
      goal or an ideal   or copyright   advertisements

4. The Greek soldiers were inspired by the messenger's **feat**.

   a. French word for   b. remarkable   c. running
      "good heart"   deed   ability

5. The **host** nation proclaims the opening of the Olympic Games.

   a. whatever   b. the nation   c. the home nation
      nation is   that pays   that welcomes
      most hostile   everyone's bills   others

SPELLING

Circle the correctly spelled word in each group.

1.	athlete	2.	plege	3.	recieve	4.	stadiam
	athalete		pledge		receve		stadium
	athleet		pleadge		receive		stadiem

SENTENCE COMPLETION

Unscramble the words from the reading to correctly complete each sentence.

1. The Olympic Games are both **ROISTHIC** _____
   and thrilling.

2. Athletes agree to participate for the **NOOHR** _____
   of their country.

3. The first **NEMORD** _____ Olympic Games were
   held in 1896.

4. The Olympic marathon race is run over an open **ROUCSE**
   _____.

DRAWING CONCLUSIONS

Use information from the reading to help you answer the questions.

1. In 1896, the winner ran the marathon
   in two hours and 58 minutes. How
   much faster did the 1996 winner
   cross the finish line?   _____

2. For how long have women athletes
   been competing in the Olympics?   _____

3. Why do you think the rings on the Olympic flag are *interlocking*?

   _____

THE IDITAROD

Before reading . . .

For more than 1,000 years, people in snowy lands have depended on sled dogs for transportation. During the early 1900s, explorers reached the North and South Poles by using sled dogs. Today, when we think of sled dogs, we think of racing. And when we think of racing, we think of the Iditarod.

The first official dogsled race took place in 1908. The race was the All-Alaska Sweepstakes. The winner completed the 408-mile course in just over 119 hours. The first race in the continental United States was held in 1917 in Ashton, Idaho.

Today, the most famous dogsled race in the world is called the Iditarod. Begun in 1973, this annual race stretches from Anchorage to Nome, Alaska. The course follows an old frozen river route and covers miles of mountain ranges and dense forests. In even-numbered years, the trail follows the 1,151-mile-long northern route. In odd-numbered years, it takes the slightly different, 1,161-mile southern route.

It usually takes from 10 days to three weeks to complete the Iditarod. The goal of most drivers is simply to finish the race. But the *best* drivers are very competitive. After all, the winning driver wins a cash prize of at least $50,000!

The Iditarod is a grueling race. Only a few dozen women have competed. But between 1985 and 1990, women won five of the six races! Libby Riddles won in 1985. Susan Butcher won in 1986, 1987, 1988, and 1990.

FUN FACTS

- The Iditarod is named after a deserted mining town along the route.

- The Iditarod commemorates a famous event in Alaska's past. It was midwinter, 1925, when a driver and his dogs undertook a dangerous emergency mission. A deadly disease called *diphtheria* was raging in Nome. Were the driver and his dogs able to deliver medical supplies in time to stop the epidemic? They were!

The Dogs

What breeds of dogs are trained as sled dogs? Alaskan and Siberian huskies are the most popular. They have strong backs, deep chests, and tough feet. Their protective coats of hair allow them to withstand temperatures as low as 60 degrees below zero!

Drivers depend on their dogs and take good care of them. Racing rules protect the hardworking animals, and a veterinarian is on call for all races.

MUSH!

Sled drivers are often called *mushers*. This is thought to come from the French word *marcher*, meaning "to march." But the command "Mush!" is hardly ever used to start the dogs. Instead, mushers yell commands such as "All right!" "Let's go!" or "Hike!"

The Equipment

The average racing sled is about eight feet long and weighs less than 40 pounds. It is equipped with a brake and usually a *snowhook*— a device that works like a boat's anchor.

The dogs wear padded harnesses and are hitched to the sled by a rope called a *gangline.* Drivers in long-distance races must take along survival items such as an axe, a sleeping bag, and snowshoes.

The driver stands on the back of the sled and holds onto the handles. He pushes the sled up hills. He also gives commands to the *lead dogs*, which run at the head of the pack.

FIVE DOGSLED EVENTS

The International Sled Dog Racing Association (ISDRA) was founded in 1966. ISDRA and the International Federation of Sled Dog Sports created racing rules and a championship program. Drivers today compete for points. Every year, the top drivers in each class receive gold, silver, and bronze medals.

- *Speed racing*, the most popular type of racing, features the fastest dogs and lightest sleds. Contestants are divided into classes, based on the number of dogs and the length of the trail. Trails are usually no longer than 30 miles.

- *Gig racing* is speed racing where there is no snow. Instead of sleds, three-wheeled carts *(gigs)* are used.

- *Freight racing* requires larger dogs to pull a sled loaded with extra weight—usually about 50 pounds of cargo per dog.

- *Weight pulling* tests strength. Dogs have one minute to pull a weighted sled 16 feet.

- *Distance racing* pits both dogs and driver against nature. Most distance trails range from 25 to 150 miles.

COMPREHENSION

Write **T** or **F** if the statement if *true* or *false.* Write **NI** if there is *no information* in the reading to help you make a judgment.

1. _____ The race called the Iditarod is held every other year.

2. _____ The first Iditarod race took place in 1908.

3. _____ Drivers in dogsled races are often called "mushers."

4. _____ The course of the Iditarod runs between Anchorage and Nome, Alaska.

5. _____ The weather in Alaska can sometimes be as cold as 60 degrees below zero.

6. _____ The International Sled Dog Racing Association meets every year in Ketchikan, Alaska.

COMPOUND WORDS

Complete each sentence with a *compound word* (one word that combines two or more smaller words). To make your compounds, choose one word from Box A and one word from Box B. Hint: You will *not* use all the words in the boxes.

BOX A			
hard	with	under	snow
trail	ice	mush	cargo

BOX B			
shoes	stand	tow	took
working	draw	out	fit

1. A driver's survival items include an axe and _____.

2. In 1925, a driver _____ a dangerous emergency mission.

3. Sled dogs must have thick coats of hair to _____ the very low temperatures.

4. Strict racing rules protect the _____ animals.

PUZZLER

Use the clues to help you complete the crossword puzzle. Answers are words that complete the sentences.

Crossword grid:

- 1 D (down)
- 2 E (down)
- 3 R (across)
- 4 G (down)
- 5 M (down)
- 6 C (across)
- 7 F (across)
- 8 B (across)
- N

ACROSS

1. A few _____ women have competed in the Iditarod.

3. The route covers mountain _____ and dense forests.

6. The _____ follows the route of an old frozen river.

7. _____ racing requires large dogs to pull about 50 pounds of cargo per dog.

8. The driver who comes in third wins a _____ medal.

DOWN

1. Iditarod is the name of a _____ mining town.

2. _____ once used dogsleds to reach the North Pole.

4. Because the Iditarod is so difficult, it is often called a _____ race.

5. The command "_____" is hardly ever used to start the dogs.

VOCABULARY

Circle a letter to show the meaning of the **boldface** words.

1. The Iditarod **commemorates** a famous event in Alaska's history.

   a. raises money for
   b. commercializes and advertises
   c. honors the memory of

2. The first race in the **continental United States** was in Ashton, Idaho.

   a. on the North American continent
   b. lower 48 states
   c. neighbor just across the border

3. In 1925, people in Nome were suffering from a diphtheria **epidemic**.

   a. irritating
   skin rash

   b. rapid spreading
   of disease

   c. disorder of the
   nervous system

4. A **veterinarian** is on call for all dogsled races.

   a. veteran
   dogsled driver

   b. official from the
   racing association

   c. doctor who treats
   only animals

SYNONYMS

First, unscramble the words from the reading. Then write each unscrambled
word next to its *synonym* (word with the same meaning) below.

MOCSANDM _____   TRAXE _____

LEYL _____   SAFOUM _____

1. additional _____   3. instructions _____

2. well-known _____   4. shout _____

ANTONYMS

Write a letter to match each **boldface** word from the reading with its *antonym*
(word that means the opposite).

1. _____ **winner**   a. despised

2. _____ **popular**   b. arid

3. _____ **usually**   c. disbanded

4. _____ **snowy**   d. released

5. _____ **founded**   e. rarely

6. _____ **hitched**   f. loser

WORD COMPLETION

Add vowels (*a, e, i, o, u*) to the words that name different kinds of equipment used in racing dogsleds. Then find the definition for each word in the reading. Write the definitions on the lines.

1. **G__NGL__N__:** _____

2. **G__G:** _____

3. **SN__WH__ __K:** _____

_____

SPELLING

Circle the correctly spelled word in each group.

1. diptheria   diphteria   diphtheria

2. competitive   competive   competetive

3. annual   annaul   annuel

4. routt   roote   route

ALPHABETICAL ORDER

List the words from the reading in alphabetical order.

mining	mush	medals	mountain
medical	mission	miles	midwinter

1. _____   5. _____

2. _____   6. _____

3. _____   7. _____

4. _____   8. _____

──── REVIEW ────

RECALLING DETAILS

Use information from the readings to help you answer the questions.

1. What two nicknames did sportswriters often call Babe Ruth?

    _____   _____

2. What powerful tennis stroke was
    not used in the first tournament
    at Wimbledon?   _____

3. What is the motto of the Olympic Games?

    _____

4. Where does the Iditarod dogsled race begin and end?

    _____

SENTENCE COMPLETION

Unscramble the words to correctly complete each sentence.

1. The Iditarod race and the tennis tournament at Wimbledon
    are both **LANUNA** _____ events.

2. The ruins of the ancient Olympic **MUSTAID** _____
    were found in Athens, Greece.

3. A **LOVELY** _____ is a return of the tennis ball
    before it hits the ground.

4. Babe Ruth's earned-run average set a record low for a
    DEDHENFLAT _____ pitcher.

56

INVENTORS AND INVENTIONS

LESSON 1: The Process of Invention

LESSON 2: The Safety Pin

LESSON 3: Two Inventive Minds

LESSON 4: Tales of Two Inventions

When you complete this unit, you will be able to answer questions like these:

■ *What's the difference between an invention and a discovery?*

■ *How does an inventor get a product* patented?

■ *What do inventors from different centuries have in common?*

■ *Do some inventions create problems as well as solve them?*

PRETEST

Write **T** or **F** to show whether you think each statement is *true* or *false*.

1. _____ Most inventors work alone rather than in groups.

2. _____ Many clever devices have been invented by accident.

3. _____ The safety pin was invented in the 15th century.

4. _____ Thomas Edison had only three months of formal schooling.

5. _____ Before the Frisbee was invented, people sometimes played catch with pie tins.

6. _____ The Wright brothers used many earlier discoveries to help them invent the first successful airplane.

Pretest answers: 1. F 2. T 3. F 4. T 5. T 6. T

THE PROCESS OF INVENTION

Before reading . . .

Have you ever had a great idea for a new invention? How do you think inventors work? This lesson will give you an overview of the process of invention.

A Bright Idea

What does it take to invent something? Curiosity about the world and a desire to satisfy a need. An inventor puts ideas and materials together to make something that didn't exist before.

Prehistoric people invented the bow and arrow to help them kill animals for food. Eli Whitney put pieces of wood and wire together to invent the cotton gin. Modern inventors have given us such marvels as computers, satellites in space, and lifesaving medical equipment.

Some inventors work alone to seek the unknown. Others work together in industrial laboratories, pooling their knowledge and skills. Some inventions come about after long years of painstaking research and experimentation. Others result from accidents. Often, an innovation cannot be credited to just one person. Television, for example, was developed through the work of many inventors over many decades.

Invention vs. Discovery

Invention is closely related to discovery. Inventors use materials and ideas to make something new. Discoverers usually find something that has always existed—but has never been seen or understood before. Thomas Edison, for example, did not invent the laws of electricity. He used his knowledge of these laws to invent the incandescent light bulb. And the Wright brothers put together many earlier discoveries in order to invent the world's first successful airplane.

In 1875, the director of the United States Patent Office turned in his resignation. Claiming that there was nothing left to invent, he recommended that the office be closed.

How Inventions Come About

Inventions often solve problems—but they also create new ones. The invention of the printing press, for example, created many more needs. Printers could print so much faster that they needed newer and cheaper kinds of paper. And metals had to be found that would make better type. James Watt's new steam locomotive created a demand for high-grade steel to make railroad rails. And the development of steel created still more opportunities for many new inventions.

War has always stimulated invention. A nation at war encourages its inventors, engineers, and scientists to devise better weapons than the enemy has. Fortunately, many inventions devised for war can be used to save as well as destroy life.

THE MARCH OF PROGRESS

Inventions bring change, and change frightens many people. In the 1830s, some people demanded an end to all inventing in the United States. They feared that new machines would rob many workers of their jobs. But during this period, inventors developed the harvester, the telegraph, the steam locomotive, the sewing machine, and the process of vulcanizing rubber.

Some helpful devices have been invented by ordinary people with extraordinary imaginations. Even people with little technical or scientific training can come up with good original ideas! A man named Hyman L. Lipman, for example, thought of attaching an eraser to a pencil. He patented this invention in 1858. And the shopping bag was invented by a grocery store owner who wanted his customers to buy more food. The paper shopping bag he patented in 1917 had cord running across the bottom and up the sides to form handles. Within eight years, he was making 10 million bags a year!

Accidental inventions have led to many products that we take for granted. For years, Charles Goodyear had tried to make rubber that wouldn't melt in warm weather. Then one day, he accidentally dropped a mixture of crude rubber and sulfur on a kitchen stove. The rubber charred badly. But at its edge, the rubber had the exact quality that he had been trying to create. Goodyear then realized that heating rubber with sulfur could make it firm.

COMPREHENSION

Use information from the reading to answer the questions.

1. What motivates an inventor to come up with something new?

   _____

2. Who invented the steam locomotive? Who first thought of
   putting an eraser on the end of a pencil?

   _____

3. What's one example of an "accidental invention"?

   _____

4. What two things had to be invented after the invention of
   the printing press?

   _____

5. What's the difference between a discovery and an invention?

   _____

   _____

ANTONYMS

First unscramble the words from the reading. Then write each word next to its
antonym (word that means the opposite).

DRUCE _____   ARGOLINI _____

BROFEE _____   THREGEOT _____

1. apart _____   3. refined _____

2. imitation _____   4. after _____

PUZZLER

Use information from the reading to solve the crossword puzzle. Answers are words that complete the sentences.

ACROSS

3. The _____ of rubber and sulfur charred badly.

4. Eli Whitney invented the cotton _____.

6. An inventor needs to have _____ about the world.

7. Inventors _____ the unknown.

8. Even nonscientists can have good, _____ ideas.

DOWN

1. Some inventions take years of _____.

2. _____ is closely related to invention.

5. High-grade _____ was invented to build railroads tracks.

6. Inventions bring _____, which can frighten some people.

VOCABULARY

Circle a letter to show the meaning of each **boldface** word or phrase.

1. Thomas Edison invented the **incandescent** light bulb.

   a. glowing with heat   b. long-lasting   c. made of glass

2. Many inventions cannot be **credited to** just one person.

   a. amount recorded as paid   b. recognized as coming from   c. all the bills charged to

3. War has always **stimulated** invention.

    a. delayed,   b. prevented,   c. encouraged,
       postponed   stopped   promoted

4. The director of the U.S. Patent Office turned in his **resignation**.

    a. bitter letter   b. halfhearted   c. notice of
       of complaint   acceptance of reality   leaving his job

5. Some inventors **pool** their knowledge and skills.

    a. sell at a   b. combine,   c. challenge each
       reduced rate   cooperate, share   other at billiards

6. Some inventors work together in **industrial** laboratories.

    a. manufacturing   b. associations   c. government-sponsored
       businesses   of hard workers   think tanks

SYLLABLES

Divide the words from the reading into *syllables* (separate sounds).

accidental	locomotive	successful	inventor

1. _____ / _____ / _____   _____ / _____ / _____

2. _____ / _____ / _____ / _____

    _____ / _____ / _____ / _____

PREFIXES

1. What prefix is used before *ordinary* to describe
   someone with an unusually good imagination? _____

2. What prefix is used before *history* to describe
   the time before history was written? _____

COMPOUND WORDS

Find a *compound word* (one word that combines two or more words) in the reading to correctly complete each phrase.

1. _____ medical equipment

2. years of _____ research

3. the Wright brothers' _____

4. steel for _____ tracks

ALPHABETICAL ORDER

List the words from the reading in alphabetical order.

products	created	quality	prehistoric	paper
developed	printers	electricity	opportunities	million

1. _____   6. _____

2. _____   7. _____

3. _____   8. _____

4. _____   9. _____

5. _____   10. _____

SPELLING

Circle the correctly spelled word in each group.

1. knowlidge   knowlege   knowledge

2. successful   succesful   successfull

3. reccomend   recammend   recommend

4. weapens   weapons   weopans

THE SAFETY PIN

Before reading . . .

It's hard for modern people to imagine life without cars, TVs, refrigerators, or airplanes. Yet people of the past lived without most of the wonderful inventions we take for granted. This lesson focuses on the story of just such an invention—the safety pin.

Walter Hunt of New York invented the safety pin in 1846. Once he got the idea, it took him only a few hours to twist a piece of wire into the familiar shape still used today. Hunt's safety pin was not history's first. The people of Italy probably used similar devices as far back as 2000 B.C. But the secret of the safety pin seems to have somehow gotten lost about 500 A.D. More than 1,300 years passed until Walter Hunt reinvented this handy device.

Obtaining a Patent

A patent is an official government document that grants a person or company the right to be the only one to make or sell a new invention. Walter Hunt obtained his patent in 1849. He submitted detailed sketches and a complete written description along with his application. Why? So the Patent Office could compare his invention to other, similar devices to make sure it was original. Even today, similar papers must accompany all patent applications.

Selling the Manufacturing Rights

This process usually takes place after a patent is issued. Walter Hunt, unfortunately, made a costly mistake with his safety pin. The very day he invented it, he sold the manufacturing rights to a friend for only $400.

Small-Scale Production

An invention must be produced before it can be marketed and sold. Walter Hunt's friend, I.W. Stewart, began making safety pins in 1846. He did this by using pliers to snip wire off of a spool. Then he bent it into the shape he wanted. At first he peddled his product door to door with a hand cart.

Large-Scale Manufacture and Distribution

After something is invented, it usually takes several years for it to be produced in great numbers. Safety pins were not mass-produced until 31 years after the first safety pin was invented! This couldn't happen until 1877, when the first machine was invented to make them automatically.

FACTS ABOUT PATENTS

A patent is the right to control the manufacture and sale of a product. This monopoly is limited in time and type. Patents are given to reward inventors for their genius.

The person entitled to a patent is one who has invented or discovered some new and useful machine, product, substance, or method. Patents may also be granted for improvements on things that have already been invented, or for original new designs or processes.

A product isn't patentable if it differs only in size or shape from a similar product. An original new *principle* must be present. That's why not every invention can be patented. Here's an example: A patent will not be granted for some change in a device that would occur to any skilled mechanic. *The true test of an invention is originality.*

It is against the law to use, sell, or make an invention patented by someone else. This crime is called *infringement.*

COMPREHENSION

Circle a letter to complete the sentence or show the answer to each question.

1. The safety pin was invented about

    a. 250 years ago.　　　b. 150 years ago.　　　c. 200 years ago.

2. What two attachments must be sent along with an application for a patent?

    a. a sketch and　　　b. a check and a　　　c. an envelope
       a description　　　　 credit card number　　　and a stamp

3. Reproducing someone else's patented product is called

    a. homicide.　　　b. forgery.　　　c. infringement.

4. In what year were safety pins mass-produced for the first time?

    a. 1846　　　b. 1849　　　c. 1877

5. The true test of an invention is its

    a. reliability.　　　b. originality.　　　c. marketability.

6. Does Walter Hunt's family still own the manufacturing rights to the safety pin?

    a. Yes.　　　b. No.　　　c. It's unclear.

SPELLING

Circle the correctly spelled word in each group.

1. government　　　goverment　　　govarment

2. simmilar　　　similar　　　similiar

3. genious　　　genios　　　genius

PUZZLER

Use information from the reading to solve the crossword puzzle. Answers are words that complete the sentences.

ACROSS

1. A patent may be issued for a new _____ or process.

5. The safety pin is a handy _____.

6. A _____ is an official government document.

7. Patents are given to _____ genius.

DOWN

2. Walter Hunt was an _____.

3. Pliers were used to _____ wire off a spool.

4. A patent is given for a new product, substance, or _____.

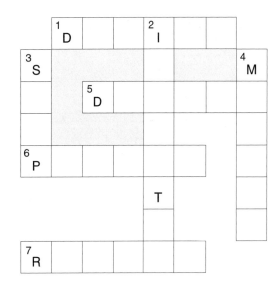

VOCABULARY

Circle a letter to show the meaning of each **boldface** word.

1. The **monopoly** guaranteed by a patent is limited.

   a. board game   b. complete control of   c. profits from

2. Detailed **sketches** must accompany the patent application.

   a. drawings   b. explanations   c. formulas

3. It is a crime to **infringe** on an inventor's legal rights.

   a. mutilate or destroy   b. sneak or look at   c. encroach or trespass on

4. Safety pins weren't manufactured **automatically** until 1877.

   a. in an auto   b. by machine   c. by human
      shop   assemblers

5. An original new **principle** must be present in an invention.

   a. the way something   b. what something   c. idea behind a
      works   is used for   government

6. The last stage of product development is large-scale manufacturing
   and **distribution**.

   a. handing out   b. offering for sale   c. dividing the
      free samples   in many places   profits fairly

7. I.W. Stewart **peddled** safety pins from door to door.

   a. biked   b. delivered   c. sold

SUFFIXES AND PREFIXES

To complete each sentence, add a *suffix* or a *prefix* to the **boldface** word.
Rewrite the word on the line.

1. Walter Hunt **(invented)** _____ the safety pin
   1,400 years after it had been forgotten.

2. Walter Hunt made a **(cost)** _____ mistake
   regarding the manufacturing rights to the safety pin.

3. A product that is only smaller than a similar product is not
   (patent) _____.

4. **(Unfortunate)** _____, Walter Hunt sold his
   rights for $400.

5. The true test of an invention is its **(original)** _____.

ALPHABETICAL ORDER

List the words from the reading in alphabetical order.

substance	twist	spool	accompany	secret
familiar	process	occur	manufacture	shape

1. _____

2. _____

3. _____

4. _____

5. _____

6. _____

7. _____

8. _____

9. _____

10. _____

NOTING DETAILS

Use information from the reading to answer the questions.

1. In what country was the safety pin *first* invented?

   _____

2. How long did it take Walter Hunt to make the first safety pin?

   _____

3. How did I.W. Stewart transport the pins he was selling?

   _____

4. How many years passed between Hunt's reinvention of the safety pin and the granting of a patent?

   _____

TWO INVENTIVE MINDS

Before reading . . .

Genius is the special power of mind and spirit that shows itself in human artistry and invention. This lesson is about two amazing people who are often called geniuses. One is a modern man, while the other lived more than 500 years ago. Both had wonderfully inventive minds.

The Great Leonardo

Born in 1492 near Florence, Italy, Leonardo da Vinci was considered the greatest figure of the Italian Renaissance. Even today, the term "Renaissance man" is used to describe someone who is skilled in many—or all—of the arts and sciences. Leonardo was a painter, sculptor, architect, engineer, and scientist. The keynote of his success in all areas was his love of knowledge and research.

Leonardo is best known for his magnificent artworks such as the "Mona Lisa" and "The Last Supper." But as an innovative scientist, he also towered above his contemporaries. He understood—better than anyone in his century or the next—the importance of precise scientific observation.

Leonardo invented a large number of ingenious machines. Many of them were potentially useful—including an underwater diving suit. He figured out a practical way to divert river water into canals for irrigation. And he is thought to have invented the *hydrometer*, a device for measuring the specific gravity of liquids. The flying devices he sketched in his notebooks embodied sound principles of aerodynamics. But Leonardo's findings were not made known in his lifetime. Most of his notebooks and drawings were not published until the 19th century.

Leonardo was truly a man who glimpsed the future. His scientific studies and inventions—particularly in the fields of anatomy, optics, and hydraulics—anticipated many of the developments of modern science. If his work had been published, it would have revolutionized the science of the 16th century.

Leonardo da Vinci was a creator in all branches of art. He was a discoverer in most branches of science. And he was an inventor in several branches of technology. No wonder he is called a "Renaissance man"!

THE RENAISSANCE

The word *renaissance* means "rebirth." It describes the dramatic revival of art, literature, and learning in Europe after the dark Middle Ages. The Renaissance occurred during the 14th, 15th, and 16th centuries.

The Wizard of Menlo Park

Thomas Alva Edison was probably the greatest inventor in history. He had only three months of formal schooling—but his inventive genius changed the lives of millions of people.

Henry Ford once suggested that the period of Edison's life (1847–1931) should be called *The Age of Edison*, because of the inventor's great contributions to the world.

Edison defined genius as "one percent inspiration and 99 percent perspiration." He demonstrated this belief by working for days at a time, stopping only for short naps.

At the age of 27, Edison set up his famous laboratory in Menlo Park, New Jersey. It was there, just three years later, that he developed the first incandescent electric light. The news astounded the world.

The 50th anniversary of that invention was celebrated in a very special way. Henry Ford moved Edison's original Menlo Park laboratory to Greenfield Village, a huge museum at Dearborn, Michigan. There, in 1929, the 82-year-old Edison re-enacted the experiment that resulted in the first electric light.

NO SUCH THING AS FAILURE

Edison refused to give in to discouragement. A friend tried to comfort him when 10,000 experiments with an early version of the storage battery failed to produce results. "But I have *not* failed," Edison insisted. "I've just found 10,000 ways that won't work."

Edison patented 1,100 inventions in 60 years. Here are a few of his best-known inventions:

1. wax paper
2. the mimeograph machine
3. the carbon telephone transmitter
4. the phonograph
5. the electric light
6. the magnetic ore separator
7. the radio vacuum tube
8. the motion-picture camera
9. the dictating machine
10. a variety of Portland cement
11. an electric vote recorder
12. a new kind of storage battery
13. the automatic telegraph machine
14. an ore-crushing machine
15. the phonograph record
16. the chemical *phenol*
17. an electrical pen
18. the three-wire electrical wiring system
19. underground electric mains
20. an electric railway car
21. a version of the stock ticker
22. the light socket and light switch
23. a method for making synthetic rubber from goldenrod plants

COMPREHENSION

Write **T** or **F** if the statement is *true* or *false*. Write **NI** if there is *no information* in the reading to help you make a judgment.

1. _____ Leonardo da Vinci and Thomas Edison were both very hard workers.

2. _____ The automaker Henry Ford was a great admirer of Edison.

3. _____ Leonardo da Vinci patented more than 1,000 inventions.

4. _____ Leonardo's wealthy family gave him the best education that money could buy.

5. _____ Thomas Edison never graduated from high school or college.

6. _____ Until Edison invented the piston engine, Ford could not have developed his automobile.

7. _____ In the 16th century, there was no such thing as "high tech."

8. _____ Thomas Edison always regretted that he couldn't draw as well as Leonardo could.

COMPOUND WORDS

Complete the *compound words* (one word made by combining two or more words) in each sentence.

1. Leonardo da Vinci is best known for his _____**works**.

2. The _____**note** of Leonardo's success was love of knowledge.

3. The bulk of Leonardo's findings were not made known during his **life**_____.

4. One of Leonardo's inventions was an **under**_____ diving suit.

PUZZLER

Use information from the reading to help you solve the crossword puzzle. Answers are words that complete the sentences.

ACROSS

4. River water can be diverted into ___ for irrigation.

5. The hydrometer is an ___ used for measurement.

7. Leonardo was born in ___.

8. The ___ ___ (two words) is a famous painting.

9. Leonardo was a painter, sculptor, architect, ___, and scientist.

DOWN

1. Edison invented the storage ___.

2. Leonardo's ___ were lost for more than 300 years.

3. Edison invented the electric light ___.

6. Edison did not believe in ___.

FACT OR OPINION?

Write **F** or **O** to show whether each statement is a *fact* or an *opinion*.

1. _____ If he had lived at the same time, Leonardo would have been a better inventor than Edison.

2. _____ Thomas Alva Edison was probably the greatest inventor in history.

3. _____ Edison was 30 years old when he invented the electric light.

4. _____ Leonardo drew many sketches of his ideas for inventions.

5. _____ Edison's laboratory was located in New Jersey.

6. _____ In a way, the early 1900s were a lot like the Italian Renaissance.

VOCABULARY

Circle a letter to show the meaning of the **boldface** word or phrase. Use a dictionary if you need help.

1. Leonardo invented many **ingenious** machines.

    a. natural, open, innocent
    b. beautiful, pleasing, popular
    c. clever, original, inventive

2. In science, Leonardo **towered over his contemporaries**.

    a. far exceeded his fellow scientists
    b. was much taller than his friends
    c. was the architect of many towers

3. Edison made **synthetic** rubber from goldenrod plants.

    a. especially stretchy and strong
    b. grown in a natural, organic way
    c. artificially created from chemicals

4. Leonardo was among the originators of the branch of physics called **hydraulics**.

    a. having to do with the mechanical properties of water
    b. science of hauling water over long distances
    c. the care and maintenance of fire hydrants

5. Leonardo made scientific studies of **optics**.

    a. optimistic thinking, a positive attitude
    b. the science that studies light and vision
    c. taking advantage of opportunities

6. Leonardo had a true love of knowledge and **research**.

    a. finding facts through careful, patient study
    b. supervising a large laboratory
    c. proving that your findings are accurate

7. Edison defined genius as "**one percent inspiration and 99 percent perspiration**."

    a. Without a great idea, hard work is all for nothing.
    b. Without hard work, a great idea won't become reality.
    c. Inspiration always causes inventors to sweat.

8. Leonardo's flying devices embodied sound principles of **aerodynamics**.

   a. spectacular stunts done with an airplane

   b. science involving sound and the sense of hearing

   c. science that deals with the forces of moving air

WORD COMPLETION

Add vowels (*a, e, i, o, u*) to complete the names of some of Edison's inventions.

1. W__X   P__P__R

2. __L __C T R __C   P__N

3. P H __N __G R __P H

4. S T __C K   T __C K __R

5. L __G H T   S W __T C H

6. R __D __ __   V __C __ __M   T __B __

SPELLING

Circle the correctly spelled word in each group.

1. sculpter
   sculptar
   sculptor

2. laboratory
   labratory
   laberatory

3. vaccum
   vacuum
   vacume

4. literature
   litrature
   litereture

SYLLABLES

Divide the words from the reading into syllables (separate sounds).

demonstrated	architect	discouragement	Renaissance

1. _____ / _____ / _____   _____ / _____ / _____

2. _____ / _____ / _____ / _____

   _____ / _____ / _____ / _____

TALES OF TWO INVENTIONS

Before reading . . .

Here are two histories of inventions that seem like they've been around forever. As you read, notice the similarities and differences between the two stories.

The Frisbee

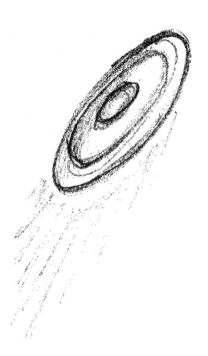

It's been 100 years since "catch the pie tin" became a campus fad at Yale and Harvard. But 50 years went by before an imaginative marketing man saw the possibilities and developed the simple game that would become an international sport played by millions of people.

In 1948, the timing was right. For one thing, plastics were just emerging as a cheap, moldable material. And for another, the public was fascinated with rumors about UFOs, Martians, or anything that had to do with outer space.

That was when a man named Walter Frederick Morrison—remembering the fun he had throwing pie tins as a boy—produced his first plastic flying saucer toy. In 1951, he introduced a new version with a center hump to suggest a spaceship's cabin. He called the new disc a "Pluto Platter" and sold it wherever he could draw a crowd—at the beach, on crowded city streets, and outside high schools.

In 1955, the owners of the Wham-O toy company saw kids playing with Morrison's discs on the beaches of Southern California. They recognized the potential of the product and made a deal with Morrison. In 1957, Wham-O began producing and selling its version of the Pluto Platter.

FRISBEES IN THE '60s: SALES SOAR

In the 1960s, Wham-O developed the first Frisbee Professional Model and sponsored Frisbee tournaments. From that effort, the International Frisbee Association was created —and Frisbees sold in the millions.

Then Wham-O heard about the old East Coast game of flinging pie tins in a game of catch. Because the first tins used were from the Frisbie Pie Company, everyone there still called the game "Frisbie-ing." Not knowing the correct spelling, Wham-O decided to rename the disc *Frisbee*—which is the trademarked spelling used today.

Earmuffs

Winters in Farmington, Maine, were cold—and so were Chester Greenwood's ears. Whenever he went ice skating, the 15-year-old's ears would get so cold that he'd have to hurry back home before they froze!

Then, one wintry day in 1873, Chester had an idea. First, he fashioned some oval loops out of baling wire. Then he asked his grandmother to sew pieces of beaver fur on the outside of the loops and black velvet on the inside. To hold the ear coverings in place, she sewed a wire connecting the loops to Chester's cap.

His idea worked! For the rest of the winter his ears stayed warm and he skated in perfect comfort. Interested neighbors soon wanted ear flaps, too. Soon Greenwood's mother and grandmother were spending all their spare time cutting, sewing, and bending wire to fill orders.

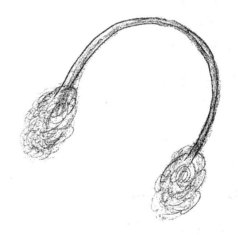

While still a teenager, Chester designed a flat steel spring to fit over the head and keep the flaps in place. It wasn't long before Greenwood's Ear Protectors were selling all over New England. He patented his design in 1877, and devised a machine to manufacture the popular new product. When he opened a factory in town, Farmington became the earmuff capital of the world—and Chester went on to become the town's leading citizen.

AN INNOVATOR AT WORK

Before Chester Greenwood died at the age of 79, he had invented more than 100 more products. Some of his inventions led to the development of modern-day airplane shock absorbers, improvements in automobile spark plugs, a new type of mechanical mousetrap, steel bows for archery, and the spring-tooth rake.

COMPREHENSION

Write **T** or **F** if the statement is *true* or *false*. Write **NI** if there is *no information* in the reading to help you make a judgment.

1. _____ The first plastic flying saucer toy was invented in 1948.

2. _____ Chester Greenwood is credited with inventing the Frisbee.

3. _____ The first ear flaps were attached to a cap with string.

4. _____ To get manufacturing rights for the Frisbee, several toy companies bid against each other.

5. _____ Walter Morrison became the leading citizen of Farmington, Maine.

6. _____ Chester Greenwood designed a machine to mass-produce his popular new product.

SENTENCE COMPLETION

Unscramble the words to correctly complete the sentences.

1. Kids were playing with the flying saucer toy on California **HABCEES** _____.

2. Chester Greenwood improved automobile **PRASK GLUSP** _____ _____.

3. When the game became a **TORPS** _____, Frisbees sold in the millions.

4. In all, Chester Greenwood developed more than 100 **DROPSCUT** _____.

5. The first earmuffs were lined with **TEVLEV** _____.

6. Greenwood **TEAPDENT** _____ his design in 1877.

7. Sometimes Morrison demonstrated his Pluto Platter on **DECWORD** _____ city streets.

PUZZLER

Use information from the reading to help you solve the crossword puzzle. Answers are words that complete the sentences.

ACROSS

1. Wham-O sponsored Frisbee ___.

3. "Catch the pie tin" was a campus ___.

4. Chester Greenwood invented steel ___ for archery.

5. Morrison's first flying disc was made out of ___.

6. In 1951, Morrison changed the design of his flying ___ toy.

7. The public had heard rumors about ___.

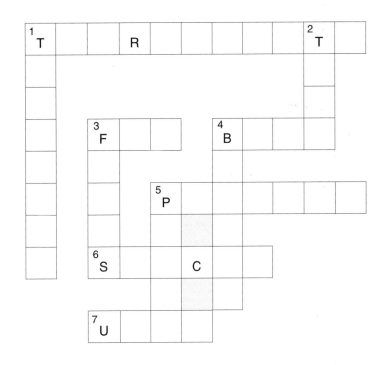

DOWN

1. Chester Greenwood was a ___ when he invented earmuffs.

2. Students enjoyed flinging pie ___ in a game of catch.

3. Interested neighbors wanted ear ___, too.

4. The outsides of the first earmuffs were covered with ___ fur.

5. Morrison called his new disc the "___ Platter."

WORD COMPLETION

Add vowels (*a, e, i, o, u*) to complete the words from the reading.

1. About 1950, the public was fascinated with _ _T_R   SP_ _C_.

2. The first step in making ear flaps was to fashion _V_ _L   L_ _ _PS out of baling wire.

3. In the 1960s, Frisbees sold in the M__ L L__ __N S.

4. Whenever he went ice skating, Chester Greenwood's __ __R S got cold.

COMPOUND WORDS

Write *compound words* (one word made by combining two or more words) to complete the sentences. Choose word parts from the box to make your compounds. Hint: You will *not* use all the words in the box.

ship	muffs	plane	trap	flaps	marked
trade	mouse	ear	air	space	planes

1. Frisbee is the _____ spelling used today.

2. Chester Greenwood invented a new type of mechanical

   _____.

3. Before long, people started to call the ear flaps _____.

4. Morrison's new disc featured a center hump to suggest the cabin of a _____.

5. Greenwood's invention led to the development of _____ shock absorbers.

VOCABULARY

Circle a letter to show the meaning of each **boldface** word.

1. Wham-O began to **sponsor** Frisbee tournaments.

   a. attend and participate

   b. organize and pay for

   c. invite and welcome

2. The Wham-O owners saw the **potential** of the new product.

   a. potency and power
   b. possibility of succeeding
   c. design improvements

3. Chester Greenwood **fashioned** some wire loops.

   a. formed and shaped
   b. made more stylish
   c. purchased from a store

4. Plastics were **emerging** as a cheap, moldable material.

   a. discovered by miners
   b. developing from paper pulp
   c. becoming known and available

5. The public was fascinated by rumors of **UFOs**.

   a. unexplained foreign objects
   b. unidentified flying objects
   c. unearthly floating orbits

ALPHABETICAL ORDER

List the words from the reading in *alphabetical order*.

toy	archery	steel	professional	imaginative
spring	citizen	spark	international	flinging

1. _____

2. _____

3. _____

4. _____

5. _____

6. _____

7. _____

8. _____

9. _____

10. _____

Unit 3 —————— REVIEW —————————

SENTENCE COMPLETION

Unscramble the words to correctly complete each sentence.

1. Sometimes **YARNROID** _____ people come

   up with great ideas for inventions.

2. Safety pins weren't **SAMS-DROPCUED** _____

   until 31 years after they were invented.

3. Leonardo da Vinci had a great love of **WONKGLEED**

   _____ and **CRASHEER** _____ .

4. The development of **CITSLAPS** _____ gave

   inventors an inexpensive new material to work with.

RECALLING DETAILS

1. What name did Walter Morrison
   give to his flying saucer toy?   _____

2. Why were most of Leonardo da Vinci's inventions not known
   during his lifetime?

   _____

3. What costly mistake did Walter Hunt make after inventing the
   safety pin?

   _____

4. What problems were created by the invention of the printing press?

   _____

HISTORIC AMERICAN PLACES

LESSON 1: Cahokia: The Mount Builders

LESSON 2: Old House and Monticello: Presidents' Homes

LESSON 3: Virginia City: Boom Town, Ghost Town

LESSON 4: Civil War Sites: A Nation Torn

When you complete this unit, you will be able to answer questions like these:

- *Who lived along the Mississippi 1,000 years ago?*

- *Members of what historic family lived in the same house for 140 years?*

- *The discovery of gold and silver had what effects on the western frontier?*

- *If you visited sites of Civil War battles, what would you see there?*

PRETEST

Write **T** or **F** to show whether you think each statement is *true* or *false*.

1. _____ The population of Nevada was multiplied by seven times in just one year.

2. _____ Monticello, the famous home of Thomas Jefferson, is located in Massachusetts.

3. _____ The largest prehistoric Native American town in the United States was established about 1,500 years ago.

4. _____ Ending America's Civil War, the Union surrendered to the Confederacy on April 9, 1865.

5. _____ A great Civil War battle was fought at Cahokia, Illinois.

6. _____ The Adams family of Massachusetts provided the United States with two U.S. presidents.

Pretest answers: 1. T 2. F 3. T 4. F 5. F 6. T

CAHOKIA: THE MOUND BUILDERS

Before reading . . .

People who lived in ancient times didn't leave a written record of the world they knew. But they did leave enough clues for scholars to make some good guesses. Read on to learn something about some early Americans.

A Peek into the Past

Just across the Mississippi River from the big city of St. Louis, Missouri, is a smaller city called East St. Louis, Illinois. These two places have been populated for a long time—since the 1700s. But just outside of East St. Louis is the site of a *much* older culture. Cahokia dates back at least 1,500 years!

The remains of the largest prehistoric Native American town in the United States has been uncovered at this site. Between 600 and 1400 A.D., from 50,000 to 60,000 dwellings were built here.

The Mound Builders

What do we know of these people who lived so long ago? Today, archeologists call these people *Mound Builders.* This general category includes various groups of Native Americans who lived at different times and had different cultures. These people are known to us by the many mounds and earthworks that are still scattered throughout the central and eastern United States.

The Mound Builders used countless baskets of earth to build their mounds. This indicates that they had a well-developed social organization. Their tools—sharp flint axes and hatchets—tell us that they could cut down trees and shape wood. Arrowheads, knives, and sharp needles made from bone have been found on these sites. They tell us that Mound Builders killed and skinned wild animals, ate their flesh, and used their pelts for clothing.

FASCINATING FACTS

Many scholars believe that Native Americans learned about mound-building from Asian peoples.

* * *

Some mounds are square, and others are round or oval. Some have flat tops.

* * *

Ohio alone has more than 10,000 mounds.

Hoes and spades show that their owners knew how to farm. We know that corn ranked as one of their main crops. And we know they raised tobacco and smoked it in beautiful stone pipes.

Evidence left behind also shows that the Mound Builders were traders. Mounds in Ohio, for example, have contained grizzly bear teeth from the Rocky Mountains, copper from the Lake Superior region, mica from New England, and shells from the Gulf of Mexico.

Archeologists have divided the mounds into two mains groups: (1) burial mounds and (2) temple mounds.

The Mississippians

Temple mounds became widespread about the year 1000. Because they were built mainly along the Mississippi River and its branches, the culture of the people who built them is called *Mississippian*.

A VISITOR FROM SPAIN

The explorer Hernando de Soto and his expedition traveled through North America from 1539 to 1542. His diaries from that period include reports of seeing temple mound people. But the era of mound-building was nearing its end. About 125 years later, the first white settlers began to arrive in greater numbers. By that time, the Native Americans had abandoned many of their old ways, and no longer built mounds.

The Native Americans called Mississippians lived mainly by farming. A religious people, they built rectangular temples made of poles and thatch. Carvings and paintings decorated the temples, and a sacred fire burned inside. Mississippians ranked among the best potters of eastern North America. Many of their arts and crafts have curious decorations of crosses, spiders, snakes, weeping eyes, and other symbols. Scholars believe that these symbols probably originated in Mexico.

A State Historic Site

Cahokia is thought to be the fountainhead of Mississippian culture. Nearly 100 earthen mounds are located there. Archeologists think these platforms were used for rulers' houses or as mortuary temples. Because it is the largest mound in the nation, Monk's Mound in Cahokia has been designated a state historic site. Monk's Mound is 1,037 feet long, 790 feet wide, and 100 feet high.

COMPREHENSION

Write **F** or **O** to show whether each statement is a *fact* or an *opinion*.

1. _____ The Mound Builders were building their mounds a thousand years before Columbus discovered America.

2. _____ Evidence shows that the Mound Builders were far more intelligent than Native Americans in the Southwest.

3. _____ If white settlers hadn't arrived, the Mississippians would probably still be building mounds.

4. _____ Monk's Mound can be found near East St. Louis, Illinois.

5. _____ Asian people brought their knowledge of mound-building over the North Pole and into America.

6. _____ The Mississippians sent riders on horseback to trade with other tribes of Native Americans.

SUFFIXES

Decide which *suffix* must be added to each **boldface** word. Then rewrite the word correctly on the line.

1. The Mississippians built **(rectangle)** _____ temples.

2. Their arts and crafts have curious **(decorate)** _____.

3. Hernando de Soto was a Spanish **(explore)** _____ who saw the Mound Builders.

4. The Mound Builders had a well-developed **(society)** _____ **(organize)** _____.

5. In Cahokia, there are nearly 100 **(earth)** _____ mounds.

6. To build their mounds, the Mississippians used **(count)** _____ baskets of earth.

PUZZLER

Use information from the reading to help you solve the crossword puzzle. Answers are words that complete the sentences.

ACROSS

1. The Mound Builders smoked beautiful clay ___.

3. By 1540, the ___ of mound-building was ending.

5. The two main kinds of mounds are ___ mounds and burial mounds.

7. Cahokia is the ___ of an ancient dwelling place.

8. A ___ fire burned inside the temple.

DOWN

2. Mound Builders used animal ___ for clothing.

4. The Mississippians were a ___ people.

5. We know that the Mound Builders were ___.

6. They built their temples of poles and ___.

SYLLABLES

Divide the words from the reading into syllables (separate sounds).

mortuary	archeologist	designated	organization

1. _____ / _____ / _____ / _____

   _____ / _____ / _____ / _____

2. _____ / _____ / _____ / _____ / _____

   _____ / _____ / _____ / _____ / _____

 UNIT 4 • LESSON 1

COMPOUND WORDS

Add *compound words* (one word made by combining two or more words) to complete the sentences. If you need help, look back through the reading.

1. Many mounds and _____ are scattered around the central and eastern United States.

2. Bone needles and _____ have been found on these sites.

3. Cahokia is thought to be the _____ of Mississippian culture.

4. Temple mounds became _____ around the year 1000.

SPELLING

Circle the correctly spelled word in each group.

1. scholars   scholers   scolars

2. hachets   hatchets   hatchetts

3. expidtion   expedition   expadition

VOCABULARY

Circle a letter to show the meaning of each **boldface** word.

1. **Mica** from New England was found in a temple mound.

   a. thin-layered mineral
   b. evidence of microbes
   c. measurable microwaves

2. **Archeologists** think the mounds were platforms for rulers' houses and temples.

   a. students of architecture
   b. scientists who study ancient peoples
   c. readers of old archives

3. Cahokia was probably the **fountainhead** of Mississippian culture.

   a. an outstanding example of

   b. the largest supplier of running water

   c. the main source of something

4. The Mound Builders include people of different **cultures**.

   a. a people's ideas, art, tools, and way of life

   b. having the highest refinement

   c. race and national identity

5. A **sacred** fire was kept burning in the Mississippians' temples.

   a. used for human sacrifices

   b. sacrilegious rites and symbols

   c. religious, holy, worthy of respect

6. The Mississippians' temples were made of poles and **thatch**.

   a. broad sheets of woven bamboo

   b. material made from straw, leaves, twigs, etc.

   c. thinly shaved strips of wood

RHYMING

Circle the word that *rhymes* with the **boldface** word from the reading.

1. **burial**   spaniel   aerial   ball

2. **known**   brown   gnome   loan

3. **hoes**   shoes   close   house

4. **build**   chilled   bruise   built

DRAWING CONCLUSIONS

Circle the word or words that correctly complete each sentence.

1. The Cahokia historic landmark is located in America's (North / Midwest).

2. The way that Mississippians built their mounds suggests that (many people worked cooperatively / different cultures helped each other).

OLD HOUSE AND MONTICELLO: PRESIDENTS' HOMES

Before reading . . .

The homes of many former U.S. presidents have been preserved as national historic sites. In this lesson you will read about two of the oldest. As you will see, each building has its own unique history.

A DISTINGUISHED FAMILY

The Adams family of Massachusetts provided the United States with two presidents. John Adams followed George Washington as the nation's second president in 1797. His son, John Quincy Adams, was elected to the presidency in 1825. Historians rank him, our sixth president, as one of the ablest men ever to hold that office.

This Old House

The Adams family has deep roots in Quincy, Massachusetts. When the first Adamses moved there, the town was part of Braintree. That was in 1688—just 18 years after the *Mayflower* brought the first pilgrims to America.

In 1787, John Adams bought an old Georgian clapboard house there. It had been built in 1731 by an East Indian sugar planter. When he bought the house, Adams was representing American interests as a diplomat in Great Britain. The next year, when he returned to the United States for good, he added several new rooms and moved in. He and his wife retired there in 1801 and lived there until his death in 1826.

John Quincy Adams and his wife Abigail—who called the family home "Old House"—made it their summer home. Then their son, Charles Francis Adams—also a Harvard-educated lawyer and U.S. diplomat—did the same. It was during his occupancy that a stone library was erected adjoining the garden.

In their turn, Charles Francis's sons spent many summers there. Both sons were Harvard-educated historians who published many books. One of these sons, Henry Brooks Adams, lived there until his death in 1927.

In all, members of the Adams family lived in the house for 140 years. If you went to Quincy today, you could tour the house, which is located at 135 Adams Street. Now designated as a National Historic Site, the Old House still contains the furnishing collected by five generations of Adamses. On a street nearby, you could also visit the historic landmark houses where John Adams and John Quincy Adams were born.

More Than a Home

Monticello is the home that Thomas Jefferson designed and built on a hilltop in Albemarle County, Virginia. The name means "little hill." But Monticello was more than Jefferson's home for more than 50 years. It was virtually his lifetime project!

A GIFTED MAN

Thomas Jefferson was the third president of the United States. He is historically distinguished as the author of the Declaration of Independence, a brilliant political thinker, and a founder of the Democratic party.

But Jefferson was a man of *many* interests. He studied music, philosophy, education, science, and farming. He carried on an immense correspondence with people all over the world. He founded the University of Virginia in 1819.

The brick Roman Revival–style house was built to his designs between 1769 and 1809. He borrowed many ideas from classical buildings he had admired in Europe. The columned portico comes from the Temple of Vesta in Rome. The centralized plan comes from the Villa Rotunda, designed by Andrea Palladio in Italy. The great dome resembles the dome of the Hotel Salm in Paris.

The house holds many mechanical devices that Jefferson invented— including a revolving desk, a dumbwaiter, and a calendar clock. And there are many inventive touches in the 35-room house itself that reveal Jefferson's remarkable architectural skill.

Jefferson was 65 when he retired from the presidency in 1809. After remodeling and making additions to Monticello many times, he had little money. In 1814, he sold his library of 10,000 volumes to Congress. Contributions from the public also aided him in his later years. But after his death in 1826, Monticello passed out of his family's hands.

Strangely enough, Jefferson died on July 4th—exactly 50 years after the adoption of the Declaration of Independence. And even more strangely, John Adams died on exactly the same day.

"All my wishes end where I hope my days will end—at Monticello."
—Thomas Jefferson

COMPREHENSION

Use information from the reading to help you answer the questions.

1. In what state is Monticello located? In what county? _____

2. Who built the house John Adams bought in 1787? _____

3. Who was the *last* Adams to live in Old House? When did he die?

   _____

4. Who was the sixth president of the United States? _____

5. Who designed his own house and filled it with his own inventions? _____

6. Which two former presidents died on the 50th anniversary of the signing of the Declaration of Independence?

   _____   _____

7. Which former president had money problems in his old age? _____

8. Which member of the Adams family added a stone library to Old House? _____

SPELLING

Circle the correctly spelled word in each group.

1. library   liberry   libary

2. pilgrims   pilgrams   pilgrems

3. volums   volumns   volumes

4. occupancy   occupency   occupantsy

PUZZLER

Use information from the reading to help you solve the crossword puzzle.
Answers are words that complete the sentences.

ACROSS

1. John and John Quincy Adams were _____ in Massachusetts.

3. Jefferson is the _____ of the Declaration of Independence.

5. Jefferson invented a revolving _____.

6. Today, you can _____ Monticello.

7. John Adams and Thomas Jefferson _____ on the same day.

DOWN

1. Jefferson's house is made of _____.

2. Jefferson moved back to Monticello when he _____.

3. The Adams library _____ the garden.

4. John Adams was the _____ U.S. president.

ANTONYMS

Choose an antonym (word that means the opposite) for each **boldface** word.
Write the word on the line. Hint: You will not use all the words in the box.

rewarded	rejection	scattered	loaned	terminated
prominent	winters	disguise	scanty	commonplace

1. **reveal** _____

2. **borrowed** _____

3. **immense** _____

4. **adoption** _____

5. **distinguished** _____

6. **summers** _____

7. **collected** _____

8. **founded** _____

SYLLABLES

Divide the words from the reading into *syllables* (separate sounds).

| correspondence | occupancy | contributions | independence |

_____ / _____ / _____ / _____

_____ / _____ / _____ / _____

_____ / _____ / _____ / _____

_____ / _____ / _____ / _____

FACT OR OPINION?

Write **F** or **O** to show whether each statement is a *fact* or an *opinion*.

1. _____ Thomas Jefferson had better taste in decorating than John Adams did.

2. _____ The Adamses occupied their family home much longer than the Jeffersons occupied theirs.

3. _____ John Adams' son called the family home "Old House."

4. _____ Today, both the Adams home and the Jefferson home are National Historic Sites.

WORD COMPLETION

Use vowels (*a, e, i, o, u*) to complete the words.

1. Five G_N_R_T_ _NS of Adamses lived in the same house.

2. When he built Monticello, Jefferson borrowed many ideas from classical buildings in _ _R_P_.

3. John Quincy Adams is ranked as one of the _BL_ST men ever to be president.

4. Thomas Jefferson was a brilliant P_L_T_C_L thinker.

5. In the 1600s, Quincy, Massachusetts, was the northern part of BR_ _ _NTR_ _, Massachusetts.

6. Thomas Jefferson invented many M_CH_N_C_L devices.

7. As a diplomat, John Adams R_PR_S_NT_D American interests in Great Britain.

8. Monticello is now a national H_ST_R_C landmark.

VOCABULARY

Circle a letter to show the meaning of each **boldface** word. Use a dictionary if you need help.

1. Charles Francis Adams was a **diplomat** for the United States.
   a. dependable congressman, automatically elected
   b. official government representative to foreign nations
   c. recipient of diplomas from several universities

2. John Adams bought an old **Georgian** house in 1787.
   a. erected during the reign of King George
   b. built by a man named George
   c. on the banks of the George River

3. Jefferson's columned **portico** was inspired by a Roman temple.
   a. front portion of a fancy roof
   b. portable grand staircase
   c. porch or covered walkway

4. Monticello was **virtually** Jefferson's lifetime project.
   a. practically or nearly
   b. having the highest virtue
   c. showing exceptional skill

5. Monticello's **dome** resembles the dome of the Hotel Salm in Paris.
   a. dominant exterior feature
   b. beautifully tiled entrance
   c. rounded roof shaped like half a globe

VIRGINIA CITY: BOOM TOWN, GHOST TOWN

Before reading . . .

Can you imagine how much things would change if the population of your state increased by *seven times* in just one year? That's what happened in Nevada between 1859 and 1860. What do you think was the cause?

THE POWER OF MONEY

Wealth from the Comstock Lode did a lot more than make a boom town of Virginia City. It also helped to build San Francisco, finance the Civil War, and make Nevada a state by 1864.

In the Middle of Nowhere

In 1859, one of the world's richest deposits of silver and gold was discovered near Virginia City. Almost overnight the small Nevada village became a bustling mining center. Named after the prospector Henry Comstock, the lode turned out to be an amazing $2\frac{1}{2}$ miles long! News of the discovery spread like wildfire. Miners and adventurers from California and the East flocked to the diggings. The population of Nevada increased from about 1,000 in 1859 to 6,800 in 1860!

Nevada's first newspaper, *The Territorial Enterprise,* was published in Virginia City. Samuel Clemens, better known as Mark Twain, and Bret Harte, the famous western writer, worked there as reporters. In 1872, Twain would publish *Roughing It*, a book describing the turbulent early days of the mining boom.

By 1861, so many settlers had moved to the mining camps that President James Buchanan took notice. As one of his final acts in office, he declared the area a separate territory. President Abraham Lincoln, who took office that same year, appointed the first governor of the Nevada

Territory. Congress enlarged the territory in 1862, and then again in 1866, when Nevada reached its present size.

In 1875, a fire destroyed most of Virginia City, but it was immediately rebuilt. By 1876, it had a population of 30,000. The booming city boasted four banks, six churches, 100 saloons—and the only elevator between Chicago and San Francisco!

Life in the Camps

Living conditions were far from comfortable. The first settlers in the mining camps lived in tents, in stone huts, or in holes in the hillsides. Prices were incredibly high since all their supplies had to be hauled over the hills from California. Lawlessness and disorder were everywhere. Many of the lonely, restless miners were gambling, gun-toting rowdies. Some miners became millionaires—but most of the others found little or no wealth.

From Boom Town to Ghost Town

In all, the Comstock Lode produced more than $300 million in high-grade ore. But by 1880, the richest mines in the area were exhausted. Virginia City quickly declined. Before long, it became a ghost town. Today, however, Nevada's largest ghost town has come back to life. Most of the town has been restored to its 1870 appearance. If you go there, you can visit Piper's Opera House and "The Castle," a Victorian mansion built in 1868 by a mine superintendent. Both historic buildings will give you a glimpse of Virginia City's former glory.

MORE GHOST TOWNS

Nevada has about 250 ghost towns. Hamilton, between Eureka and Ely, once had a population of about 15,000. The city is now completely abandoned. Rhyolite, near Beatty, had 8,000 residents in the early 1900s. Just a few buildings stand there today. The Bottle House in Rhyolite houses a museum of desert relics. How did the building get its name? It was built from thousands of beer bottles cemented together with adobe.

WHERE DID VIRGINIA CITY GET ITS NAME?

Virginia City lies in the Virginia Range of the Sierra Nevada Mountains. To get there, you would drive about 23 miles southeast of Reno.

COMPREHENSION

Use information from the reading to help you answer the questions.

1. In 1859, what valuable metals
   were discovered in Nevada? _____

2. Where was Nevada's first newspaper published? What was the
   name of the newspaper?

   _____

3. In 1860, how many people lived in
   the Nevada Territory? _____

4. Who appointed the first governor
   of the Nevada Territory? _____

5. When was Nevada named as a state? When did the state
   reach its present size?

   _____

6. What city in California profited
   from Nevada's silver and gold? _____

7. What happened to Virginia
   City during the 1880s? _____

8. About how many ghost towns can
   be found in Nevada today? _____

SPELLING

Circle the correctly spelled word in each group.

1. prospector   prospecter   prospectar

2. govenor   governor   govaner

3. finanse   finance   fineance

4. superintendent   superintendant   superendtendent

PUZZLER

Use information from the reading to help you solve the crossword puzzle.
Answers are words that complete the sentences.

ACROSS

1. In the 1880s, Virginia City became a ___ town.

4. The bottles making up the house were cemented with ___.

7. Henry Comstock was a ___.

9. Virginia City quickly became a mining ___.

10. The ___ was 2½ miles long.

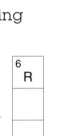

DOWN

2. There were 100 ___ in Virginia City.

3. A ___ of silver and gold was discovered in 1859.

5. In the 1860s and 1870s, Virginia City was a ___ town.

6. A museum of desert ___ is in the town of Rhyolite.

8. Wealth from the mines helped pay for the ___ War.

PREFIXES AND SUFFIXES

Add a *prefix* or a *suffix* to each **boldface** word. To correctly complete the sentences, rewrite the words on the lines.

1. After the fire, Virginia City was quickly **(built)** _____.

2. Because many miners were rowdies, **(lawless)** _____ was everywhere.

3. Some miners became **(million)** _____.

4. Congress **(large)** _____ the Nevada Territory in 1862.

5. The Comstock Lode was one of the world's **(rich)** _____ deposits of silver and gold.

6. Two **(history)** _____ buildings will give you a glimpse of Virginia City's glory days.

SYNONYMS AND ANTONYMS

First unscramble the words from the reading. Then write each word next to its *synonym* (word that means the same) or its *antonym* (word that means the opposite).

SHOGT _____	**READCLED** _____
STELSERS _____	**GAINMAZ** _____
NICLEED _____	**SUBGLINT** _____
DERSTROE _____	**HEWLAT** _____

1. **riches**

   SYNONYM: _____

2. **contented**

   ANTONYM: _____

3. **sluggish**

   ANTONYM: _____

4. **spirit**

   SYNONYM: _____

5. **named**

   SYNONYM: _____

6. **abandoned**

   ANTONYM: _____

7. **astonishing**

   SYNONYM: _____

8. **growth**

   ANTONYM: _____

VOCABULARY

Circle a letter to show the meaning of the **boldface** word. If you're not sure, use context clues for help or check a dictionary.

1. Wealth from the Comstock **Lode** helped to make Nevada a state.

   a. a huge amount; a tremendous load
   b. metal ore in seams and cracks in rock
   c. nuggets and bags of gold dust

2. There are desert **relics** in the Rhyolite museum.

   a. objects that remain from the past
   b. artwork and photographs
   c. examples of plants and animals

3. The miners' supplies were **incredibly** expensive.

   a. of very poor quality
   b. fair, under the circumstances
   c. almost unbelievably overpriced

4. A mine superintendent built a **Victorian** mansion.

   a. in the vicinity of Virginia City
   b. styled after the reign of Queen Victoria
   c. displaying his victory over poverty

5. Mark Twain wrote about the **turbulent** early days of the mining boom.

   a. calm, peaceful
   b. wild, exciting
   c. terrible, disgusting

SYLLABLES

Divide the words from the reading into *syllables* (separate sounds).

| adventures | elevator | abandoned | territory | overnight |

1. _____ / _____ / _____   _____ / _____ / _____

   _____ / _____ / _____

2. _____ / _____ / _____ / _____

   _____ / _____ / _____ / _____

CIVIL WAR SITES: A NATION TORN

Before reading . . .

About 150 years ago, the Southern states demanded recognition as an independent Confederacy. The Northern states were resolved to preserve the Union. What followed was a tragic chapter in our nation's history.

April 12, 1861—Fort Sumter Attacked!

America's Civil War began when Southern troops bombarded Fort Sumter in South Carolina's Charleston Harbor. After a 34-hour assault, the federal garrison surrendered, and the nation was plunged into civil war.

Four years later, when the Confederates evacuated the fort, it was little more than rubble. In 1947, Fort Sumter was declared a national monument. Today, much of the old military post has been excavated. A museum stands on the site. Tour boats carry visitors to the fort from downtown Charleston.

September 17, 1862—The Bloodiest Battle

Confederate General Robert E. Lee was desperate to move the war up to the North. Moving up from Virginia, some 41,000 rebel soldiers took up battle position at Sharpsburg, Maryland, near Antietam Creek. But at dawn on September 17, Union forces launched an artillery attack. The battle raged all day over an area of 12 square miles. At dusk, when the battle ended, 12,410 Union soldiers and 10,700 Confederate soldiers had been killed or wounded.

The bloody battle gave the Union an unexpected victory and marked a major turning point in the war. It gave President Abraham

The Civil War split the United States into two camps. By the time it ended, it had taken more than 500,000 lives and ruined millions of dollars worth of property.

Lincoln the opportunity to issue the preliminary Emancipation Proclamation five days later.

Today, the battlefield at Antietam is marked with about 200 tablets and monuments that memorialize the bloodiest battle of the Civil War.

April 3, 1865—Lee Withdraws from Richmond

Five Forks Battlefield lies 12 miles west of Petersburg, Virginia. It was there, on April 1, that Union troops cut Robert E. Lee's last supply line in his defense of Petersburg and Richmond. This marked the end of the 10-month campaign to take Petersburg, and it was one of the last battles of the Civil War. Richmond was doomed when Petersburg fell on April 3. Lee's surrender was now inevitable.

Many original earthworks used in the campaign are still visible. Today, many visitors come to the Five Forks Battlefield National Landmark and Petersburg National Battlefield. They often go to see the Poplar Grove National Cemetery, which is located nearby. Many of the Civil War dead are buried there.

April 9, 1865—The South Surrenders

Robert E. Lee's veteran forces were starving and badly outnumbered. At last Lee realized that further combat would be in vain. So he sought a meeting with Union Gen. Ulysses S. Grant. The surrender took place in the Wilmer McLean House in Appomattox, Virginia.

The original structure was dismantled in 1890. But it has now been rebuilt on its original site. Other buildings, including the nearby courthouse, have also been restored to their appearance in 1865.

Just five days after Lee's surrender, President Abraham Lincoln held his last Cabinet meeting. That very evening he was assassinated by John Wilkes Booth.

COMPREHENSION

Use information from the reading to answer the questions.

1. Which Union general accepted
   Robert E. Lee's surrender?   _____

2. Why did Robert E. Lee lead his soldiers into Maryland?

   _____

3. Where did America's Civil War begin?

   _____

4. What remnants of the Civil War
   can still be seen in Petersburg?   _____

COMPOUND WORDS

Complete each sentence with a *compound word* (one word that combines two or more words) from the reading.

1. Tour boats leave from _____ Charleston.

2. The _____ at Appomattox has been restored.

3. The Five Forks Battlefield is now a national _____.

4. When Petersburg fell, Lee's forces had to _____
   from Richmond.

FACT OR OPINION?

Write **F** or **O** to show whether each statement is a *fact* or an *opinion*.

1. _____ Civil War sites aren't very interesting to visit, because
   there's so little to see there.

2. _____ If he had had fresh troops available, Lee could have
   continued the war.

3. _____ The Civil War lasted almost exactly four years.

4. _____ An army that has no way to get supplies is in big trouble.

5. _____ The Civil War might have been avoided if America's leaders had been better negotiators.

6. _____ More than 23,000 soldiers were killed or wounded on September 17, 1867.

PUZZLER

Use information from the reading to help you solve the puzzle. Answers are words that complete the sentences.

ACROSS

2. The battle at Antietam raged from dawn to _____.

4. The Union's _____ to take Petersburg lasted 10 months.

6. The attack on _____ Sumter started the Civil War.

8. Soldiers from the _____ fought for the Confederacy.

10. The _____ took place in the Wilmer McLean House.

DOWN

1. Union troops cut off Lee's _____ line in his defense of Petersburg and Richmond.

3. Fort Sumter is located at the _____ in Charleston, South Carolina.

5. Soldiers from the _____ fought for the Union.

7. Richmond was _____ when Petersburg fell.

9. Five Forks Battlefield lies 12 miles _____ of Petersburg.

SYNONYMS

Unscramble the words from the reading. Then write each word next to its *synonym* (word with the same meaning).

DNEED _____   TIES _____

ORTSOP _____   MEETCRYE _____

NAWD _____   SENDFEE _____

1. **protection** _____   4. **soldiers** _____

2. **sunrise** _____   5. **concluded** _____

3. **location** _____   6. **graveyard** _____

VOCABULARY

Circle a letter to show the meaning of the **boldface** word or phrase. If you need help, look for context clues in the sentences or check a dictionary.

1. Southern troops attacked the federal **garrison** in Charleston.

   a. warehouse full of ammunition   b. a fort and the soldiers in it   c. house of government representatives

2. After Petersburg fell, Lee's surrender was **inevitable**.

   a. unavoidable   b. in jeopardy   c. infinite

3. Lee realized that further combat would be **in vain**.

   a. pure vanity   b. vengeful   c. useless

4. Lee's **veteran** troops were starving and outnumbered.

   a. new recruits   b. experienced   c. middle-aged

5. Union forces launched an **artillery** attack near Sharpsburg.

    a. hand-to-hand combat
    b. bombs dropped from airplanes
    c. mounted guns, such as cannons

6. About 200 **tablets** and monuments can be found on the battlefield at Antietam.

    a. flat pieces of stone inscribed with words
    b. small, flat, hard cakes of medicine
    c. pads of writing paper

ALPHABETICAL ORDER

List the words from the reading in alphabetical order.

wounded	**battle**	**restored**	**dismantled**	**visitors**
position	**rubble**	**combat**	**monuments**	**rebel**

1. _____

2. _____

3. _____

4. _____

5. _____

6. _____

7. _____

8. _____

9. _____

10. _____

SPELLING

Circle the correctly spelled word in each group.

1. cematary   cemetery   cemetary

2. Charleston   Charlestown   Charlston

3. Petersberg   Petersburg   Peterburg

4. memoralize   memorylize   memorialize

— REVIEW —

PEOPLE AND PLACES

Unscramble the words to complete the sentences.

1. Ancient **VANITE CRANEAIMS** _____

   _____ built **PLEEMT** _____ mounds

   and **LIARBU** _____ mounds.

2. Thomas Jefferson's home, **NOILTEMLOC** _____,

   contains the **RADCLEAN** _____ clock he invented.

3. Many Civil War **TABFLETSLIDE** _____ have been

   preserved as national **SKRAMNALD** _____.

4. Discovery of the **MOCKCOST DEOL** _____

   _____ made Virginia City a **OMBO NOWT** _____

   _____.

COMPREHENSION

Circle the words that correctly complete the sentences.

1. The (Mississippians / gold prospectors) were a religious people.

2. Mark Twain once worked in (Charleston / Virginia City).

3. The state of (Nevada / Massachusetts) has about 250 ghost towns.

4. The bloodiest battle of the Civil War was at (Fort Sumter / Antietam Creek).

5. (Thomas Jefferson / John Quincy Adams) wrote the Declaration of Independence.

GLOSSARY OF READING TERMS

adapted rewritten to be made shorter or easier to read

alliteration repetition of the initial sound in two or more words; a poetic device

analyze to identify and examine the separate parts of a whole

author's purpose the writer's specific goal or reason for writing a particular book, article, etc.

categorize to divide into main subjects or groups

cause a happening or situation that makes something else happen as a result

classify to organize according to some similarity

compare to make note of how two or more things are alike

compound word word made by combining two or more smaller words

conclusion the end or last part of a novel, article, etc.

context clues the words in a sentence just before and after an unfamiliar word or phrase. Context clues help to make clear what the unfamiliar word means.

contrast to make note of how two or more things are different from one another

describe to tell or write about something or someone in detail in order to help the reader or listener create a mental image

details bits of information or description that support the main idea and make it clearer

dialogue lines spoken by characters in a story or play

discuss to talk or write about a topic, giving various opinions and ideas

effect the reaction or impact that occurs as a result of a cause

elements the essential parts or components of a whole

excerpt section quoted from a book, article, etc.

fact something that actually happened or is really true

fiction literary work in which the plot and characters are imagined by the author

figurative language colorful, nonliteral use of words and phrases to achieve a dramatic effect

generalize to form a general rule or idea after considering particular facts

graphs charts or diagrams that visually present changes in something or the relationship between two or more changing things

homonyms words pronounced alike but having different meanings and usually different spellings

identify to name or point out; to distinguish someone or something from others

image idea, impression; a picture in the mind

inference conclusion arrived at by careful reasoning

interpret to explain the meaning of; to figure out in one's own way

judgment a decision made after weighing various facts

literature the entire body of written work including fiction, nonfiction, drama, poetry, etc.

locate find; tell where something is

main idea the point or central thought in a written work or part of a work

multiple-meaning words lookalike words that have different meanings in different contexts

nonfiction writing about the real world, real people, actual events, etc.

objective reflecting what is actual or real; expressed without bias or opinion

order items arranged or sequenced in a certain way, such as alphabetical order or order of importance

organize to put in place according to a system

outcome the result; the way that something turns out

parts of speech grammatical classifications of eight word types: adjective, adverb, conjunction, interjection, noun, preposition, pronoun, or verb

passage section of a written work

plot the chain of events in a story that leads to the story's outcome

plural word form showing more than one person, place, or thing

point of view the position from which something is observed or told; when a character tells the story, *first person* point of view is used; an author who tells the story in his own voice is using *third person* point of view.

predict to foretell what you think will happen in the future

prefix group of letters added at the beginning of a word to change the word's meaning or function

recall to remember or bring back to mind

refer to speak of something or call attention to it

relationship a connection of some kind between two or more persons, things, events, etc.

scan to glance at something or look over it quickly

sequence items in order; succession; one thing following another

singular word form naming just one person, place, or thing

subjective reflecting personal ideas, opinions, or experiences

suffix group of letters added at the end of a word that changes the word's meaning or function

symbol a concrete object used to represent an abstract idea

table an orderly, graphic arrangement of facts, figures, etc.

tense verb form that shows the time of the action, such as past, present, or future

term word or phrase with a special meaning in a certain field of study such as art, history, etc.

tone the feeling given by the author's choice of language

vocabulary all the words of a language